The Friendship Book

of Francis Gay

D1632205

D. C. THOMSON & CO., LTD.
London Glasgow Manchester Dundee

A Thought
For Each Day
In 1984

Links of gold may dull and sever,
but links of friendship last for ever.

EARLY PROMISE

When warm sunny days are only a dream
And the frost lies heavy on meadow and stream,
One day it happens—you give a glad shout:
" Come quick and look—the snowdrops are out!"

JANUARY

SUNDAY—JANUARY 1.

THE Lord bless thee, and keep thee: the Lord make his face to shine upon thee, and be gracious unto thee.

MONDAY—JANUARY 2.

MAYBE some people think it a bit old-fashioned, but I imagine that a great many of us still make what we call New Year Resolutions. If we examine them, however, I think we shall find that many of them consist of resolving *not* to do in the future something we have been guilty of doing in the past.

I think it would be much better to resolve to do something we have *not* done in the past—to attempt something fresh and different. Most lives tend to get into a bit of a rut sometimes and it might do us a world of good to read a different newspaper, try a fresh holiday resort, take up a new hobby, take a different route or a different means of transport on some familiar journey.

Little things perhaps—but they really could put " newness " into the New Year.

TUESDAY—JANUARY 3.

THE late Rev. Phillips Brooks, an American preacher of a few generations ago, was famous for his inspiring sermons but even more so for his deeds of gentleness and mercy. This, surely, was because he lived out one of his own dictums: " Duty makes us do things well, but love makes us do them beautifully."

THE FRIENDSHIP BOOK

A LL over the world the New Year is celebrated with ceremonies of one kind and another — feasts, the ringing of bells, the wearing of new clothes, the giving of presents, and so on.

In China, the making of special dumplings called Jiaozi is a very popular New Year custom, particularly among children. The dumplings are arranged in large, flat baskets, but the exciting thing for the children is that hidden in the dumplings are coins—in much the same way that we used to put sixpences and three-penny bits in Christmas puddings.

This is really a very appropriate New Year symbol. Sometimes there is a certain amount of foreboding as we wonder what the year will bring. How much better if we could greet it eagerly as the Chinese children do with their New Year dumpling, looking for the *good* it holds.

P ART of the charm of many country villages lies in the thatched cottages, barns, inns and sometimes even schools and churches. I have often admired the designs on some of these roofs but I did not realise till recently that they often bear the " trademark " of individual thatchers. Some thatchers will put on the top of the roof a straw model of, say, a bird or a dog, to proclaim their handiwork.

All this, and the mason's marks on the stones of old buildings, show justifiable pride in work well done. And why not? We can't all be craftsmen, but no matter how humble the task, if we do our best we can share something of their satisfaction and pride and leave our mark in a job well done.

THE FRIENDSHIP BOOK

WHEN Victor Hugo, the French writer, was exiled to the island of Jersey, ill and persecuted, it is said that each evening he used to climb to a nearby cliff-top and sit quietly meditating as he gazed across the water. Then he would pick up a pebble—sometimes large, sometimes small—throw it resolutely into the water below, then walk away with springing step.

Someone who had observed this habit for a long time at last plucked up courage to ask, " Monsieur Hugo, why do you come here day after day to throw stones into the water?"

Hugo gazed at his questioner for a moment, and then said, " Not stones, my friend. I am throwing my self-pity into the sea."

The sea ... a lake . . . the bottom of the garden—it doesn't matter where you throw it. Just get rid of it!

HAVE you heard this old verse before? It has a lot to say . . .

Kind friends, have you heard of the town of No Good, on the banks of the River Slow,
Where the Some-time-or-other scents the air, and the soft Go-easies grow?
It lies in the valley of What's-the-use? in the province of Let-her-slide;
It's the home of the reckless I-don't-care, where the Give-it-ups abide.
The town is as old as the human race, and it grows with the flight of years,
It is wrapped in the fog of the idler's dreams,
Its streets are paved with discarded schemes,
And are sprinkled with useless tears.

PLACE OF PRAYER

The artist, the craftsman,
*   Both increase*
Holy joy
*   And inner peace.*

SUNDAY—JANUARY 8.

HE is the Rock, his work is perfect: for all his ways are judgment: a God of truth and without iniquity, just and right is he.

MONDAY—JANUARY 9.

A GROUP of schoolchildren were visiting London and were given tea on the terrace of the House of Commons which enjoys a superb view overlooking the Thames.

"Well, what do you think about this?" asked their teacher.

There was silence for a moment and then a 13-year-old lass piped up: "The tea's a bit strong, Miss!"

TUESDAY—JANUARY 10.

I HAVE on my bookshelves a volume of children's stories written by the late Rev. Dr James Black, and I often dip into its pages. If you wonder why a grown man should be reading children's stories the explanation lies in the Dedication at the front of the book:

> "*How old are you?*"
> "*I am seven years old.*"
> "*Then I write my book for you.*"
> "*How old are you?*"
> "*I am seventy years young.*"
> "*Then I write my book for you.*"

Seven years old or seventy years young—these are not ages; they are attitudes. What they have in common are simplicity, open-mindedness, enthusiasm, affection, hope, trust. Truly these are the keys to full and happy living.

THE FRIENDSHIP BOOK

NOT only among children but among adults too I have noticed that scrapbooks, which went through a long period of neglect, seem to have recovered a certain amount of popularity.

The subjects vary, of course, according to individuals and their particular interests. Some will collect pictures of sporting personalities — golfers, footballers, tennis players and so on. Others specialise in local history or in architecture—pictures of churches and castles. There is really no end to the possibilities.

I once knew a man who made a scrapbook intended for looking at in times of worry and tension. All the pictures were of quiet and gentle subjects—a sleeping child, a cottage garden, a placid pool, a country church, a quiet woodland. He gave the pictures simple titles: " Still Waters ", " Repose ", " Silent Forest ", " Peace ", and so on.

He told me once that simply turning over the pages and meditating on the quiet scenes brought a great sense of tranquillity.

It's an idea I am glad to pass on.

LITTLE Susan heard an appeal for toys to be given to a home for underprivileged children. She very carefully went through her collection of toys and dolls and, to her mother's surprise, put aside nearly all her best dolls to be sent to the home. The only one Susan was keeping was a battered old doll which had an eye missing on one side and an arm on the other. When asked for an explanation, the little girl came up with the uncontradictable reply: " Nobody else would love a poor little thing like this."

LONDON PRIDE

Sure as her river, surging on its way,
The city's heart beats ever, night and day.

THE FRIENDSHIP BOOK

WISDOM, humour and pathos—all these, from time to time, come " out of the mouths of babes ". Here are a few of my favourite stories.

A middle boy of three brothers complained to his mother, " Mummy, you are always saying, ' You two big boys . . . ', or, ' You two little boys . . . ' and I *always* get caught!"

A small girl asked for a light to be left on when she went to bed. " There is no need to be afraid of the dark," said her mother. " I'm not afraid of it," she retorted, " but it gets in my eyes and I can't see anything!"

Another little girl proudly brought home her school report with a mark of 97% for music.

" That's a splendid mark," said her mother.

" Yes, I know," was the reply. " Even Sir John Barbirolli could only have got three more if he'd been in our form!"

DURING a busy morning rush hour, folk were swarming on to a bus and struggling to find seats.

In the midst of the struggle, the conductor's voice rang out: " There is plenty of room if you will only just move up and be nice."

When you stop to think of it, there's a lot of sense in that, isn't there? Nothing is ever lost by simply moving up and being nice.

HE took them up in his arms, put his hands upon them, and blessed them.

B

A PREACHER visiting a country church was asked if he would like any particular hymn to be sung to agree with his sermon.

"No, no," he replied. "As a matter of fact, I hardly ever know what I am going to say until I arrive in the pulpit."

"Oh, well, in that case," said the vicar, "perhaps we had better have the hymn ' For those at sea '."

I ONCE read a lovely legend of a mother who lost her son in battle. She was inconsolable. " If only I could see him again," she prayed, " even for just five minutes." An angel answered her prayer: " You will see him for five minutes," he promised, but he quietened the woman's eagerness by adding, " Think a minute. He was a grown man and you have thirty years of his life to choose from. How would you like to see him? As a soldier, dying heroically at his post? Or as you last saw him, when he left to join his unit? Would you like to see him at his last prize-giving when he stepped on to the platform to receive his honours?" The mother's eyes lit up at pride remembered. " Or would you like to see him as a babe in your arms?"

The mother shook her head, and quietly said: " No, I would have him for five minutes, as he was one day when he ran in from the garden to ask me to forgive him for being naughty. He was so small and so unhappy, and the tears were making streaks down his grubby face. He flew into my arms, small and helpless."

The moments she wished most to relive were those when her son had his greatest need of her.

THE FRIENDSHIP BOOK

MY friend Andrew has a wife whom he loves very much. If she has a fault it is that she is just a little house-proud. One result of this is that Andrew is the best-trained foot-wiper I have ever seen.

I walked up the road with him the other night and he asked me in. I was on the point of making a little joke about his foot-wiping ritual and then I checked myself as a thought came into my head.

When we wipe our feet at the door, perhaps we are brushing away not only mud and dust but leaving behind any grudge or bad temper we stored up during the day.

Let's try to leave behind us
Not just the dust of town,
Let's buckle on a cheerful face
And brush away the frown,
So on the mat we leave behind
All thoughts bitter and unkind.

THIS morning I received a communication from the Inland Revenue. It reminded me of the citizen of the newly-independent republic of Zimbabwe who received a similar communication from the Commissioner of Income Tax.

He looked at it, and then replied as follows: " I have to refer to the attached form. I regret so grave I am unable to complete the form as I do not know what is meant by filling this form. However, I am not interested in this income service. Could you please cancel my name in your books, as this system has upset my mind and I do not know who registered me as one of your customers."

I wouldn't try it if I were you!

KEEPING ON

Every worthwhile thing we do
Must call for effort, you'll agree,
And hard as the endeavour proves
So greater the reward will be.

FRIDAY—JANUARY 20.

THERE are times when most of us, oppressed by the rush and turmoil of life, express the wish, as we put it, " to get away from it all " for a while.

This isn't a new idea, for the Roman Emperor, Marcus Aurelius, who lived in the 2nd century, wrote a famous book, *Meditations,* in which he said, " Men seek retreats for themselves, houses in the country, seashores and mountains . . . but nowhere, either with more quiet or more freedom from trouble does a man retire than into his own soul."

Wise words indeed! Today, as in the time of Marcus Aurelius, it is possible for us to " get away from it all " not by some long journey into some remote place, but by withdrawing into ourselves in quietness, prayer and meditation. As Jesus said, " When you pray, go into a room by yourself, shut the door, and pray to your Father who is there in the secret place."

SATURDAY—JANUARY 21.

TWO hundred years or more after it was written, John Wesley's rule, if followed, would make the world a happier place today:

> *Do all the good you can*
> *By all the means you can,*
> *In all the ways you can,*
> *In all the places you can,*
> *At all the times you can,*
> *To all the people you can,*
> *As long as ever you can.*

SUNDAY—JANUARY 22.

A WORD spoken in due season, how good is it!

MONDAY—JANUARY 23.

OUR neighbours have a young nephew who has adopted us and often drops in to see us when he visits his aunt and uncle. He is very fond of riddles and usually has a new one for us when he calls. Here are two of his latest offerings:

" Mr Gay, why did the man tiptoe past the medicine cabinet?" I had to confess I did not know. " Because he did not want to waken the sleeping tablets," came the answer.

Then, another day: " Why did the golfer wear two pairs of trousers?" Again, I didn't know. " In case he got a hole in one!"

TUESDAY—JANUARY 24.

CHRISTINE'S grandfather could be relied upon to help when things went wrong. When she was twelve someone stole her new bicycle during the brief time she left it unguarded; she failed by a few marks the entrance examination to the new school of her choice; her best friend moved away. On top of everything else she was ill during the summer holidays!

Afterwards she went to her grandfather's home in the country to recover. She arrived feeling depressed and sorry for herself.

" Why does everything go wrong for me?" she complained.

" I don't know," Grandpa replied, " but there are some things I *do* know and I'll tell you one of them, Christine. The wood for the best violins is taken from the windward side of the tree because it's the side that suffers most that produces the finest wood. Think on it, lass."

She did—and felt much better as a result!

MANY of my readers have no doubt heard the Breton Fishermen's Prayer: " Protect me, my Lord, my boat is so small, and your ocean so big." From the same source, but probably less familiar, are the words: " O God, I know that I am not worthy to attain to your beautiful heaven. Please let me just stay here."

That last sentence is an impossible request, of course, but these two prayers seem to me to capture two qualities sorely lacking in modern life — simplicity and a sense of wonder. We cannot, and should not want to put back the clock of progress; all the same, amid the growing complexities of our civilisation we do well to pray Rudyard Kipling's prayer: " Teach us delight in simple things."

We should never take for granted the marvel and mystery of the world about us. To keep our sense of wonder is to find life endlessly surprising and satisfying.

THURSDAY—JANUARY 26.

SOMETIMES, when we are ill or worried, it's hard to think of others. But an old lady I know manages this very well despite the fact that she has been confined to a chair for many years. The first thing she does when she has visitors is to ask how *they* are and what *their* news is.

Her polite concern for others, which we all need to share, is summed up in this old and rather amusing prayer:

> *Make me, dear Lord, polite and kind*
> *To everyone, I pray,*
> *And may I ask you how you find*
> *Yourself, dear Lord, today?*

GEORGE FREDERICK WATTS, the famous painter, is perhaps best known for his picture "Hope", now in the Tate Gallery. It shows a lonely, blind figure sitting on top of the world, listening to the one unbroken string of a lyre.

Although his work brought him fame and fortune, G. F. Watts set little store by material things. He often quoted, as his motto:

What I spent, I had;
What I saved, I lost;
What I gave, I have.

SATURDAY—JANUARY 28.

I THINK there should be snow every week. There's nothing like snow for breaking the ice."

It was maybe an odd way to put it, but I knew exactly what Willie Johnston meant.

There had been a tremendous fall of snow overnight and it looked as if the pavement would be dangerous, especially for old folk.

But in no time at all, six of us were out with shovels, including a couple who had recently come to live in the neighbourhood and had scarcely had the chance to speak to anybody.

Soon the pavement was clear and we were all leaning on our shovels, talking away.

Yes, as Willie said, it broke the ice all right. None of us will be sorry if there's another fall and our work has to be done all over again!

SUNDAY—JANUARY 29.

PRIDE goeth before destruction, and an haughty spirit before a fall.

MONDAY—JANUARY 30.

PEOPLE have always been fascinated by fire and its origins. Perhaps one of the quaintest legends about fire is the Scandinavian one telling how Thor made the first fire by striking his own head with a hammer!

I like John Oxenham's faint suggestion of fire worship when he says, " Kneel always when you light a fire." Well, nowadays it may well be gas and electric fires, or central heating we use, but when I draw the curtains on a cold winter night, I sometimes recall that old myth about Thor and feel how, in a very real sense, we may think of warmth as a gift of the gods!

TUESDAY—JANUARY 31.

WHEN the Lady of the House and I were on holiday on the island of Iona, we bought a small jug which took our fancy. Inside it, on impulse, I placed a tiny pebble which I had picked up on the beach—just a simple reminder of a delightful holiday.

Then, quite by chance, shortly after we arrived home, I came across Robert Gibbings's account in *Sweet Thames Run Softly* of a man who collected stones and used to say as he looked lovingly at his collection, " Flowers fade, timber crumbles, metal corrodes, but these stones will remain." It is good sometimes, amid chance and change, to have a reminder of lasting things.

But Robert Gibbings mentions yet another aspect of stones. " Few people realise," he says, " the beauty of even the commonest of stones, yet the insect who makes his home in a pile of gravel on the roadside lives in a palace."

Truly, there is glory in the commonplace if we have eyes to see it.

FEBRUARY

WEDNESDAY—FEBRUARY 1.

WHAT do we all need most? William James, an American professor, had no doubts on the matter. When at the end of term the young ladies of his class presented him with a beautiful azalea, he wrote them a delightful letter of thanks, in which he said: " The deepest principle of human nature is the craving to be appreciated."

James was a very famous philosopher who wrote many profound books but I'm sure he never wrote anything truer than those words.

We all need appreciation as flowers need the sun. The boy who brings the papers, rain or shine; the apprentice at his bench; the new girl at the hairdresser's; the bearer of the morning cup of tea.

Oh, we say we don't expect to be thanked—but isn't it nice when we are!

THURSDAY—FEBRUARY 2.

YEARS ago, in the days of travelling tradesmen of one kind and another, a passer-by noticed an umbrella repairer at work by the road-side. He watched him for a little while and then commented on the quality of his work.

" Yes, I try to do a good job," was the reply.

" Well, I suppose it pays you to do that, for when you come round the next time."

" It's not just that," said the man. " I may never be in this neighbourhood again, but if I do a good job I make it easier for the next fellow who comes along. People will have a good impression of umbrella men."

We, too, can make it easier for others to follow us.

A FRIEND was telling me how her family used to make fun of her because she was in the habit of sitting down on Friday evening with a sigh, saying, " What a week!" Then she began to realise that it really wasn't funny. She found that she was, in fact, tending to concentrate just on the things that had gone wrong during the week.

She remembered reading about someone who, at the end of every day, used to write in the square for each day of her monthly calendar the day's " highlight "—something to be glad and grateful about. So she thought she would give it a try. It worked! " The difficulty," she said, " was in picking out just *one* thing from so many in each day."

She still has a week-end phrase, only now it is, " What a wonderful week!"

R EGINALD FOORT, the organist, used to say that most people, if they fell forward, put up their hands to protect their faces, but, he went on, " My instinct is to put my hands behind me to protect them, for they are a precious possession on which my livelihood depends."

I have heard of musicians, artists and others, insuring their hands for large sums of money. But then, aren't *all* our hands of great value? This is true not only in terms of the use we make of them in a multitude of ways for ourselves, but in our relationship with others—the helping hand, the friendly wave, the warm handshake, the confidence we can give through its firm grip to a little child or a blind person.

There is wealth in your hands and mine!

ONCE UPON A TIME

Those first exciting steps in reading
Open up a wonderland,
Offering to lucky children
Magic kingdoms to command.

THE FRIENDSHIP BOOK

IF God so clothe the grass of the field, which today is, and tomorrow is cast into the oven, shall he not much more clothe you, O ye of little faith?

FOR over 30 years Dora Oliver was the water bailiff on a stretch of the River Dove in Derbyshire—a job in which she followed her father. She used also to be a concert pianist but arthritis in her hands put an end to that.

But she still has her music. Walking along the river bank with a television interviewer she paused and said, " Listen to that weir! How it sings!"

" Sings?" queried the interviewer.

" Yes," she replied. " Everything makes music if people have ears to hear . . . the river, the breeze, the reeds. There's music everywhere."

All we need are ears to hear and hearts in tune with the beauty of the world about us.

ONE might not perhaps expect to find an Old Celtic Blessing printed on the stationery of a commercial firm but that is indeed where a correspondent found the following:

> *May your needs be granted,*
> *May your health improve,*
> *May happiness surround you,*
> *May your spirits gain strength.*

The letter was about a purely business transaction, says my correspondent, but it was lifted to a higher plane by that simple blessing. May those same words transform *your* work today!

IN the early years of the Industrial Revolution with all its social problems, young John Bright had his own personal grief—the death of his wife. His friend Richard Cobden sympathised with him as best he could, and then said to Bright, " There are thousands of homes in England at this moment where wives and mothers and children are dying of hunger. When the first grief is past I would advise you to come with me and we will never rest till the Corn Law is repealed."

And so it was. As John Bright worked to ease the sorrows of others, so he found his own grief healed and soothed.

THE windows in the Lady Chapel of Liverpool's Anglican Cathedral are all concerned with women—women of the Bible, women saints, and women who played a great part in local and national life right up to modern times.

Many of them are household names, familiar to us all, but one medallion concerns a woman perhaps less well known, whose life has always impressed me greatly. She was Kitty Wilkinson, the wife of a working man. He earned only about a pound a week, but during their lives they saved 45 orphans from the workhouse, bringing them up in their own home. Her great work for the city was done during the cholera epidemic of 1832 when she not only acted as a nurse in the poorest and most wretched dwellings, but started a laundry where the clothes of the disease-stricken families were washed and disinfected.

Kitty Wilkinson was surely what a poet has called one of the heroes and heroines of common life.

OUR local church, week by week, has a helpful " thought " on its Wayside Pulpit board. Here are a few which have appeared during the past month or two:

"*To get joy, you must give it; to keep it you must scatter it.*"

"*One believing heart sets another on fire.*"

"*Do not make God your pillow, or prayer your eiderdown.*"

"*It's the storm that proves the strength of a ship.*"

"*We see things not as they are, but as we are.*"

SATURDAY—FEBRUARY 11.

PERCY SHAW hadn't much money in his younger days. He was one of a large family brought up in a then bleak Boothtown, Halifax.

One foggy night while motoring from Bradford to Boothtown, the visibility became so poor that he had great difficulty in seeing the way. Below the road was a sheer drop, protected by a fence and only the gleaming eyes of a cat sitting on the fence saved him from going over the edge. This gave Percy Shaw the idea of experimenting with the road studs which he called " cats' eyes ". It took several years to persuade the authorities of their value and he had even to arrange at his own expense the first " try-out " at a well-known danger spot near Leeds.

Even then nothing much happened. It was the wartime blackout that put the studs on the road to fame and with them their inventor. Yet these life-savers might just have dimmed away in an old Boothtown factory had not Percy Shaw believed in the maxim, " Never give up."

SUNDAY—FEBRUARY 12.

THE eternal God is thy refuge, and underneath are the everlasting arms.

MONDAY—FEBRUARY 13.

THE President of the Transport and General Workers Union needed his hair cut, and visited a certain barber in Coventry.

The barber chatted away to him, principally about the crisis in industry and transport, and refused to change the subject even when the other tried to do so.

" Why are you so interested in the transport crisis?" asked the President.

" I'm not," replied the barber. " But it's so much easier to cut your hair when it's standing on end!"

TUESDAY—FEBRUARY 14.

THERE has been a revival in recent years of sending greetings and cards on St Valentine's Day. Back in Victorian times these cards were often very elaborate and expensive—not to say ingenious. One popular type had a little tab at the side so that when you pulled it the lady or gentleman on the card winked an eye! Another had a miniature musical box which played a love song.

All this is a long way from the real St Valentine, who, tradition says, lived in the 3rd century. He appears to have been remembered as a Christian for his good deeds to his fellows and for his martyr's death. Perhaps we tend sometimes to dismiss St Valentine's Day as a bit of sentimental folklore but love to one another and love to God are qualities this world badly needs, and it is in the power of each of us to supply them—not only on St Valentine's Day but every day.

WEDNESDAY—FEBRUARY 15.

I DON'T like the cold. It makes me feel miserable—and, if I'm honest, a bit bad-tempered at times! It was on such a day that the Lady of the House hunted out, for my special benefit, a quotation she had come across about the Eskimos. It was by a writer, Gontran de Poncin, who had spent much time living with them. He wrote:-

" Here was a people living in the most rigorous climate in the world, in the most depressing surroundings imaginable . . . shivering in their tents in the autumn, fighting the recurring blizzard in the winter, toiling and moiling fifteen hours a day merely in order to get food and stay alive. Huddling in their igloos through this interminable night, they ought to have been melancholy men . . . instead, they were a cheerful people, always laughing, never weary of laughter."

Well, I found it difficult to complain about the cold after that! But doesn't it just go to show that the important thing is not our circumstances but how we react to those circumstances.

THURSDAY—FEBRUARY 16.

I SUPPOSE most of us have periods when worries tend to keep us awake at night. When I have that experience I try to remember the American bishop, William Quayle, who said that one night when he was pacing his bedroom, worried and sleepless, God said to him, " Quayle, you go to bed. I'll sit up the rest of the night!"

Whimsical? Slightly irreverent, even? Well, perhaps so. But what a great point it makes . . . the God who " shall neither slumber nor sleep ", who " guardeth our sleeping and our waking ".

C

THERE once was a boy whose pet hate at school was Latin. He loved reading, though, and through his books he developed a love of history, especially in Roman times. So, he set to and mastered Latin—because he wanted to write a book. Today, 200 years later, his book is still available, and still read. It is " The Decline and Fall of the Roman Empire ", described as one of the foremost historical works of all time.

Its author was Edward Gibbon, the schoolboy who had once hated Latin.

OUR old friend Mary is almost entirely house-bound, but she never lets it get her down. Those of us who visit her find her cheerfulness stimulating and infectious and come away feeling the better for having been in her company.

She is a great reader, but I confess I was a little surprised to find her one day with a volume of Tennyson's poetry on her lap.

" I'm glad you've come, Francis," she said. " I thought you would be interested in this for your *Friendship Book*. Listen!"

She opened the book at a page she had marked with a slip of paper, and read:

She spies the summer through the winter bud,
She tastes the fruit before the blossom falls,
She hears the lark within the songless egg,
She finds the fountain where they wailed ' Mirage '.

" Isn't that wonderful?" said Mary, her eyes lighting up.

It certainly is, and I think I know a bit more now about the secret of Mary's cheerfulness.

THE FRIENDSHIP BOOK

WHITHER thou goest, I will go; and where thou lodgest, I will lodge: thy people shall be my people, and thy God my God.

YEARS ago I jotted down in one of my note-books a verse by an anonymous writer, probably of the early 16th century. I have often turned to it for inspiration and it may help you, too:

> *Thou shalt know Him when He comes*
> *Not by any din of drums,*
> *Nor the vantage of His airs,*
> *Nor by anything He wears,*
> *Neither by His crown,*
> *Nor His gown.*
> *For His presence known shall be*
> *By the holy harmony,*
> *That His coming makes in Thee.*

ALTHOUGH death is a subject which many people shrink from thinking or talking about, a positive and hopeful philosophy towards it is of great value.

Such a philosophy was given by Mark Guy Pearse when he described it as a house: " We go in at the back door, and come out at the front door. We go in blind, we come out seeing celestial beauty. We go in deaf, we come out hearing celestial music. We go in dumb, we come out singing the songs of the redeemed. We go in halt and maimed and old and decrepit, and we come out young and strong to run with joy the shining way."

A wonderful house!

WINDMILLS—particularly working ones—are such a rare sight nowadays that when we *do* come across one I imagine most of us get quite a thrill. In the year 1400 there were about 10,000 mills spread up and down the country and I was interested to read recently in an article on the subject that in mediaeval times the miller ranked third in line to the lord of the Manor and the parish priest—with tithes and dues to match his position.

Perhaps that is why the so-called " Jolly Miller " who lived by the River Dee felt he could afford to say,

I care for nobody, no not I
And nobody cares for me.

What a silly man he must have been! Whatever his wealth and position, he had obviously not learned that life consists in caring and being cared for. If we have someone to care for and someone who cares for us, we are wealthy indeed.

VISITING Malhamdale in Yorkshire the Lady of the House and I were caught in one of those sudden and torrential downpours of rain for which the area is well-known. We sheltered in a barn and the farmer who was working there told us an interesting story.

Nearby is the village of Airton and nearly 300 years ago a local linen-weaver, William Ellis, left a house and land for a Quaker Meeting House—a token of his deep spiritual concern. But he made another bequest, too—" six large coats and six women's hoods " were to be provided and loaned out to travelling Friends who were caught in rough weather.

I like that concern for body, as well as for spirit!

A CERTAIN Methodist minister had a son who was training to be a lawyer, and who was at home one Sunday morning when his father felt unwell and unable to conduct the morning service.

The budding lawyer was asked to deputise. He objected, saying that he had no sermon, and no time to prepare one. However, his father insisted it would be good practice for him, and surely he could talk on religion for about 25 minutes.

So, after spending a short while in his father's study, the young man went across to the chapel to conduct the morning service. Soon afterwards, his father, feeling a little better, popped into a back pew in order to listen to his son's sermon. Later, his son asked him what he thought of it. " I was quite ashamed," declared the minister bluntly. " Your delivery wasn't bad, but the subject matter was extremely poor."

His son nodded. " I didn't think much of it either, but it was the best I could find among the big pile in your study."

WHEN things go wrong, don't complain,
Pick up the threads and start again.
For over there the sun is shining,
Look up and find the silver lining.
Throw back the shutters of despair,
And let the rays of hope shine there.

IT shall be, if he call thee, that thou shalt say, Speak, Lord: for thy servant heareth.

GOOD FRIENDS

MONDAY—FEBRUARY 27.

CANBERRA, the capital of Australia, is reputed to have over eight million trees. Many of them are flowering varieties so the beauty of the city can be imagined. Partly this is thanks to a government decision to give every new householder some shrubs and trees when they build a house. But it is also due to the work of a 19th century rector of St. John's Church there, the Rev. P. Galliard Smith, who planted seeds wherever he went . . . a reminder to us, surely, that it is not just the " powers that be " who have a responsibility for creating a better world; each of us can play our part.

TUESDAY—FEBRUARY 28.

I THINK these words of " A Nurse's Prayer " from Fiji are lovely:

Lord, use my hands; they are not scarred like Thine,
  They have not felt the tortures of the Cross:
But they would know upon their palms
  Thy touch, without which all their work is loss.

Lord, use my hands, that some may see, not me,
But Thy Divine compassion there expressed,
And know Thy peace, and feel Thy calm and rest.

WEDNESDAY—FEBRUARY 29.

JULIE MASON of Wokingham was a typical mum. She had three children, two of whom were not yet old enough to go to school. One day her husband arrived home to find the house in chaos. " What on earth's been happening?" he asked critically.

" You're always wondering what I do all day," replied Julie. " Well, *today I didn't do it.*"

MARCH

THURSDAY—MARCH 1.

ALL over the world today, Welshmen will be wearing a leek or a daffodil and celebrating the occasion of St David's Day. David, born towards the end of the 5th century, was a saintly man who lived a very simple life. As with all saints, many legends have gathered about him and his work, but it is fact not fiction that I like to remember about him.

The rule of the monasteries he founded was very strict and such property as they had was held in common. Even the absent-minded use of a phrase such as "my bed", "my book", "my spade" brought a penance on the speaker.

Of course, that kind of strictness would be unworkable in our modern world—but wouldn't we all be happier if we could learn to say "me" and "my" and "mine" just a little less often?

FRIDAY—MARCH 2.

POETS in every age have sung the wonder of springtime.

Shakespeare reminds us that "sweet lovers love the spring", Swinburne tells us that "blossom by blossom spring begins" and George Herbert writes of "Sweet spring, full of sweet days and roses."

But it is a modern writer, Sam Churchill, who for me has best captured the spirit of springtime: "Spring is a gentle stirring deep inside that insists you walk instead of waiting for a bus. It's when you breathe deeply. It's that fleeting moment of time each year when you suddenly become you. It's when you say 'Good Morning' and mean it."

THE FRIENDSHIP BOOK

A LOCAL church had organised a Self-denial Week, and the members of one family were discussing how they would respond. Father said he would stop smoking for a week and give the money to the church; Mother said she would give up chocolates, and the daughter of the house promised to forego her weekly visit to the cinema. The young son of the family thought for a moment and then he said, " I'll give up rice pudding. I never did like the stuff anyway!" Not quite the right idea, was it?

If, during Lent, or at any other time we decide on some act of self denial, we might well remember the words of David in the Bible, " I will not offer unto the Lord that which has cost me nothing."

B LESSED are the poor in spirit: for theirs is the kingdom of heaven.

THE author who writes under the nom-de-plume of " Miss Read " has delighted thousands of readers with her account of village life in books such as *Village School* and *Return to Thrush Green*.

Some time ago she was asked to name her favourite village in England, and she chose Peasmore in Berkshire where, many years before, she had spent just over two months as the acting-headmistress of the tiny village school.

She admitted that there were many very lovely villages in the area where she now lives. " So why do I choose modest Peasmore as my favourite village? The answer is simple. *I was happy there.*"

TUESDAY—MARCH 6.

THE Lady of the House and I find immense pleasure in walking round the gardens of some of the " stately homes " of our land but when we think of the problems a gardener can have with even a small plot of ground we sometimes wonder how these are coped with on a large scale.

Mr Charles Simmons is Head Gardener at Blickley Hall in Norfolk and after the severe winter of 1981/82 he was asked by a visitor how the gardens had fared. He admitted that some plants had been damaged and some had died and he pointed out areas of devastation. But he was not in despair. " We're knocked back, but not knocked out," he said.

A good phrase and one I hope we can apply to ourselves when we get setbacks on the road through life.

WEDNESDAY—MARCH 7.

I DON'T vouch for the truth of it but there is a story that during the War years an inexperienced farmer in East Anglia complained to a neighbour that the Government had ordered the branding of all livestock.

" I know," said the other. " Have you done it?"

" Yes," said the farmer, " I've got it done—but I had an awful lot of trouble with the bees!"

THURSDAY—MARCH 8.

THE warm and sunny days, no doubt,
Are still a long way off.
There may be snow, high winds may blow,
I splutter, sneeze and cough.
But days are stretching, some birds sing—
I'll manage to survive till spring!

THE FRIENDSHIP BOOK

JOHN RUSKIN, the 19th century art critic and writer, once pointed out that the constituents of common mud could well be sand, soot, clay and water—the very substances from which precious gems such as sapphires, diamonds, emeralds, rubies and the rest are formed.

It's rather a startling reminder isn't it, about how glory is found in the commonplace. What transformations are possible in us and in our world!

DR STANLEY JONES, an American by birth, spent most of his working life as a Methodist minister in India and as Principal of the Sitapur Boarding School.

His books, which include *The Christ of the Indian Road, Christ at the Round Table, Christ and Human Suffering* and *Victorious Living,* have made him widely known and brought much inspiration to thousands of people in this country.

But behind one of his books is a little-known story. For years he had made notes in the margin of a copy of the New Testament hoping that one day they would become the basis of a book. Then that New Testament was stolen and it seemed that his years of work had come to nothing.

He wrote: " To begin all over again to make new notes—a heart-breaking task! But I had to do it and now I find that it was the best thing that could have happened to me. My New Testament is richer and so am I for having lost the old notes."

Truly, the courage " to begin again " when failure or frustration face us can be one of life's most rewarding experiences.

SUNDAY—MARCH 11.

ALL the ends of the world shall remember and turn unto the Lord: and all the kindreds of the nations shall worship before thee.

MONDAY—MARCH 12.

THE secretary of a village church once received a letter from the TV Records Office addressed to "The Present Occupier" of the church and wondering why there was no record of a TV licence?

The secretary replied: "The Present Occupier is God. He took up residence in 1876 when His House was opened and consecrated. As He is an all-seeing God, He really has no need for a television set."

TUESDAY—MARCH 13.

WHEN her friends knew that Marie Sklovodska was to be married one of them offered to pay for her gown as a wedding gift.

Marie, who was very poor, gratefully accepted the offer but added that she would like one " practical and dark " so that it could be worn for her work.

A strange request, you may think, but Marie was no ordinary bride. She was to marry Pierre Curie and her work was in the laboratory where the two Curies were to form one of the most famous and successful partnerships in history.

Together they discovered radium and not only gave birth to a new science but provided mankind with new hope for treating a dreaded disease.

The marriage was a very happy one and when Marie Curie died in 1934, another famous scientist said of her: " Marie Curie is, of all celebrated beings, the only one whom fame has not corrupted."

THE FRIENDSHIP BOOK

A LOCAL Council official was making house-to-house calls to find out how many were living in a certain district. When he enquired at one house as to how many people lived there the mother of the house began, " Well, there's Horace, and Jim, and Nelly and Mary and—" The official interrupted, " I don't need names, madam. I just want numbers."

" They haven't got numbers," the woman retorted indignantly. " They have all got names!"

I WONDER if you share the same delight as I do when I pick up a book from a second-hand counter and find certain passages underlined by a previous owner.

A small book I came across the other day had these sentences heavily marked:

" I had rather feel compunction than know the definition thereof.

" If thou knowest the whole Bible by heart, and the sayings of all the philosophers, what would it profit thee without the love of God and without grace?"

These words were written 600 years ago by Thomas à Kempis. Thomas was the son of a poor workman in Germany. At the age of 20 he entered a monastery and during the next 70 years he copied precious manuscripts and set down his own thoughts in such books as " The Imitation of Christ ".

This book has been translated into hundreds of languages and in the opinion of many, ranks second only to the Bible. The thoughts of this humble monk, written all these centuries ago, still retain all their old power to advise and inspire.

TIME FOR TEA

A life of dedication
From the flesh may set us free,
Yet the spirit may be strengthened
By a welcome cup of tea . . .

FRIDAY—MARCH 16.

THE other day I read again the Biblical story of King David's kindness to the son of his great friend Jonathan, and it made me wonder how much store people set by the promises of others.

I like the definition of one small boy who said: "To promise means to keep it in your mind, keep it in your mind, keep it in your mind—*until you do it*."

SATURDAY—MARCH 17.

WHEN Rudyard Kipling was a small boy, one of the joys of his life was to visit his Aunt Georgina who lived in a great house in London. At the gate of the house was an iron bell-pull and having rung the bell he had to wait to be admitted. Those waiting moments he described as being of indescribably joyful anticipation. So much so that in later life he begged to have, and received, that bell-pull for his own house, so that boys who visited him might share the thrill of anticipation he had enjoyed.

What an important part of life anticipation is! I know some people who never make any arrangements for their holidays, but just set off. They argue that the thrill of the unknown and unexpected is their reward. Well, so be it. But I think that they miss the greater thrill of anticipation. Looking forward to things is a very real part of enjoyment, whether it be a holiday, a meal, meeting with friends, or an evening by the fireside. Long live the art of eager and joyful anticipation!

SUNDAY—MARCH 18.

BETTER is a dinner of herbs where love is, than a stalled ox and hatred therewith.

MONDAY—MARCH 19.

THOMAS FULLER, the 17th century clergyman-author, told an anecdote about West Yorkshire's Martin Frobisher, the Elizabethan Admiral. He had brought back a very large but soft stone from one voyage believing that it contained either gold or silver. It proved worthless.

" Yet," observed Fuller, " will no wise man laugh at his mistake, because of such experiments they shall never hit the mark who are not content to miss it."

James Graham, the 1st Marquis of Montrose, had something of the same idea:

> *He either fears his fate too much*
> *Or his deserts are small,*
> *Who will not put it to the touch*
> *To win or lose it all."*

And even more brief is the old motto: " Nothing venture, nothing win."

TUESDAY—MARCH 20.

IT is said that when Stanley Baldwin was elected Prime Minister his friends gathered round to congratulate him, but he said to them quietly, " It is not your congratulations I need, but your prayers."

There must be times when the affairs of the nation and the world fill us with near-despair and we wonder what possible difference anything we do can make. But remember how Paul urged that, " petitions, prayers, requests and thanksgivings be offered to God ... for kings and all who are in authority."

To remember in our prayers those who bear the almost intolerable burden of government is one of the ways in which we can all play our part in the life of the world.

THE American poet and preacher, Henry van Dyke, once said, " The first day of Spring is one thing, and the first Spring day quite another." Well, I suppose he was right; there may be several weeks between them!

Yet, whatever the weather, the first official day of Spring ought to lift our spirits with hope. As Margaret Elizabeth Sangster wrote:

Never yet was a Springtime
When the buds forgot to blow.

There, indeed, is a thought for today!

THURSDAY—MARCH 22.

THERE is an old Cornish legend which tells of five brothers who all had big bushy beards. One day two of the brothers decided to shave off their beards, but two others said they preferred to keep theirs on. The fifth brother couldn't make up his mind whether to shave or not to shave. The unbearded brothers urged him to take it off and be like them, the bearded brothers begged him to keep it on.

Both sides argued with him and each other, until he just didn't know what to do. In the end, to try to please all his brothers, he shaved *one* side of his face only.

Well, of course that didn't please them either! In trying to please everyone he had succeeded in pleasing no-one at all.

We are all faced with difficult decisions at one time or another and sometimes, sadly, others are offended by what we decide to do. But if it's the right course to take then we must have the courage to go ahead. Better that than sitting on the fence and going nowhere.

D

FRIDAY—MARCH 23.

DR SAMUEL JOHNSON'S father used to run a bookstall at the weekly market in Uttoxeter. On one occasion he wasn't feeling well and asked his son if he would look after his stall for him. Samuel refused and this refusal haunted his conscience for nearly 50 years. He then returned to the Market Square in Uttoxeter to do penance.

Of course there wasn't a bookstall to man any more, so the now famous Dr Samuel Johnson stood there, in the pouring rain, for most of the day, without his hat, as a sign of remorse and regret.

SATURDAY—MARCH 24.

THE Lady of the House and I were fascinated when we came across a blacksmith in a village through which we were passing on holiday; and his conversation was as fascinating as his work.

" Do you know why the blacksmith's leather apron has a fringe?" he asked us. We had to admit that we had not even realised that, traditionally, the apron had a fringe.

The blacksmith told us that, according to legend, when Solomon's Temple was completed the workmen were feasted and the blacksmiths protested because they were left out.

" You did no work in the building of the Temple," they were told.

" But we made the tools for the workmen," was the reply.

So Solomon relented and said that a blacksmith was to come to the feast and that as a mark of honour he should have a fringe on the edge of his leather apron. Every blacksmith since has been entitled to the same.

THE FRIENDSHIP BOOK

FOR wisdom is better than rubies; and all the things that may be desired are not to be compared to it.

THE minister was paying a pastoral call on one of his flock, and remarked that he hadn't seen her in church lately.

"No," came the straightforward reply. "My daughter is learning to play the harp—and I am having second thoughts about going to heaven!"

ONE of the great explorers of our day is Lt. Colonel John Blashford-Snell, who by his own intrepid adventures has become a legend in his own life-time.

Some years ago he and his party made contact with a New Guinea tribe who had never before seen anyone from the outside world. He was asked, in a television interview, how an approach was made in a situation like this. In answer, he produced a tiny plastic gadget which, when the button was pressed, produced the recorded sound of human laughter! This, he said, brought the immediate response of laughter from those who heard it, thus establishing friendly contact at once.

We don't need the gadget; we can smile, we can laugh. And what a great cementer of human relationships it is! As Robert Louis Stevenson said, "That people should laugh is a better preparation for life than many other things higher and better-sounding in the world's ear."

BEFORE the Second World War, a woman called Mrs Berwick was in charge of the Salvation Army's social work in Liverpool. Eventually she retired and went to live in London.

Then war came and with it the air-raids. Although she was retired, all Mrs Berwick's impulse to help others sprang to the surface again. She assembled a first-aid kit, hoarded her tea supplies ready for making " cuppas " when required, and put a notice in her window: " IF YOU NEED HELP, PLEASE KNOCK HERE."

I'm not suggesting we should all put up notices like that, but what a lot it means to us to *know* that there are others to whom we can always turn for help, and what a lot it might mean to others that they could similarly turn to *us*.

SOME time ago I read in a springtime gardening article these words which have stuck in my mind: " The first flowers are twice themselves for *being first*."

And indeed, what joy they bring after the cold, bare, winter days!

I think we can find a lot of happiness in keeping our eyes and ears alert for " firsts ". We all know about the first cuckoo of spring, but what about the first glimpse of a new moon, the scent of the first mowing of the grass, the first moments of a new day, the first day of a new week, the first page of a new book!

Life is full of these ordinary, everyday " firsts " if we only look for them, and they can give a new excitement to our lives.

FRIDAY—MARCH 30.

FRAU HEINZ was a displaced person who had once been a professor of music in Dresden.

A minister in a nearby town had given her permission to play his piano—but she felt she couldn't go on her own. Then a friend, the Dutch religious writer, Corrie ten Boom, mentioned her own love of music, and accompanied the professor to the minister's home.

The piano was battered and old—its strings rusted, and keys missing. It looked impossible to raise much of a tune on it. However, Frau Heinz asked Corrie to suggest something for her to play. Corrie found herself asking for Bach's " Chromatic Fantasy " — and immediately wished she had thought of something less difficult for a tired old woman and a battered old piano. But the professor's eyes gleamed with delight—and in seconds her skilful fingers were extracting from that battered piano a flood of beautiful music.

The old lady hadn't had to leave *everything* behind when the war broke out. She had taken her most prized possession with her—her music, for " that which is in your heart can never be taken from you."

—Isn't that so true of life?

SATURDAY—MARCH 31.

FEW of us have the capacity, or even the desire, to be great in the way that the world uses this word, but there is a kind of greatness we can share and which can give us a lot of satisfaction. It is set forth in the words of an anonymous writer: " He is not greatest who has the greatest number of servants, but he is greatest who serves the greatest number."

FRIENDLY LIGHT

APRIL

<u>SUNDAY—APRIL 1.</u>

IN some places Mothering Sunday is still known by another name, Refreshment Sunday. Why? Because this Mid-Lent Sunday allowed a break in the long and strict fasting period before Easter. Apprentices and servant girls who worked at a distance were allowed to visit their homes, often taking with them gifts or flowers or the traditional Simnel cake.

A happy custom and a reminder to us that though life has its disciplines and duties, it also offers us many breaks and pleasant interludes. For these we should be truly grateful.

<u>MONDAY—APRIL 2.</u>

MRS IRENE WINSTONE of Swansea sent me this poem with a message:

There's always something to wreck your day,
Something obstructive to mar your way,
A thought to change blue skies to grey—
  If you let it.

There's always something to spoil your fun,
Disturb your mind when the day is done,
A cloud that threatens to hide the sun—
  If you let it.

Ignore what upsets you—the stones, the stings—
Find something good in whatever time brings;
Life will surround you with wonderful things—
  If you let it!

IN his later years, the great French artist, Pierre Auguste Renoir, suffered severely from arthritis which affected his hands so badly that it was only with the greatest difficulty that he could hold a brush. He struggled on bravely with his painting in spite of the pain.

A friend once asked him why he continued to paint when the physical agony was so great. Renoir replied, " The pain passes, but the beauty remains."

And surely there is a philosophy here which can be applied to many difficult situations in our own lives.

WEDNESDAY—APRIL 4.

THIS is the story of a brave little boy.

One spring evening I walked around the cathedral close at Norwich trying to find the grave of Edith Cavell, the courageous Norwich nurse of the First World War who was shot for helping Belgians to escape. A cathedral guide soon came to my rescue, and as we stood by the grave, she told me of how, recently, a small boy from the cathedral school had been running in the quiet precincts and had accidentally knocked over and broken the cross on the grave.

He could have said nothing about it for nobody had seen him, but with thumping heart he went and told the headmaster what he had done. A new cross was made for the grave.

" That boy will go far," said my guide. " He will grow up to do what he counts as right, whatever the cost."

Edith Cavell, and now this little boy, both fought fear—and won.

THE FRIENDSHIP BOOK

ALMOST any public clock in Britain could stop without the fact being noted anywhere except in the immediate local area, but when Big Ben stops (as it did a few years ago for 13 hours due to mechanical breakdown) that is national news. Someone at the time called Big Ben " the most loved and reassuring sound in Britain ".

There have been other occasional stoppages—through a flock of starlings, the weight of snow on the hands, and even a workman getting his foot in the way of the hands!

For many of us one of the most moving associations of Big Ben was the institution of the Silent Minute, when the bell started striking again after World War II, and for millions of listeners to BBC radio, nine o'clock each evening became a period of silent prayer. I know that there are still many who find inspiration in that " loved and reassuring sound ", the chiming of Big Ben.

THE 19th century English scientist, Professor T. H. Huxley, once wrote about coming home after a considerable stay on the continent. He said, " I reached Folkestone on a rainy day. The streets of that little southern town were thick with mud, but I could have lain down and rolled in it; I was so glad that it was English mud!"

Well, I can't help wondering what Huxley would have done if someone had challenged him to be as good as his word! Yet perhaps it was a pardonable exaggeration to express the joy we must all have felt at some time in returning to whatever place it is that we call home.

SATURDAY—APRIL 7.

PROFESSOR T. R. Glover, the historian and religious writer, used to love to tell the story of a small girl arguing with her sister and saying, "Barbara, the Bible does *not* end with Timothy. It ends with Revolutions."

How right she was! Many of us know what a change its truths have made in our own lives, and the difference those truths could make to the world if we would all take them seriously and act on them.

SUNDAY—APRIL 8.

GO to the ant, thou sluggard; consider her ways, and be wise.

MONDAY—APRIL 9.

ALTHOUGH the annual Spring Bulb Festival at Spalding in Lincolnshire with its flower-bedecked floats processing through the streets is a breathtakingly beautiful spectacle, I used to feel a little uneasy about the millions of tulip heads being used in this wasteful way. Then I learned something which I had never realised before.

The plants are grown at Spalding not principally for the flowers but for the bulbs, and the bulbs can only be satisfactorily produced by removing the heads of the flowers! Clearly it is better to use them to give pleasure to thousands of people at the festival than merely to take off the heads and let them rot on the ground.

It made me wonder how often we make judgments, as I had done, without knowing the full facts. What a lot of wisdom there is in these two words, " Judge not "!

MOST of us are encouraged when we discover that great and gifted people often share some of our own follies and foibles. I felt a good deal of sympathy with Dr Lloyd Douglas, the author of many books including " The Robe " and " The Big Fisherman ", when I read a delightful incident of his domestic life told by one of his daughters.

Dr Douglas was very short-sighted and when, without his glasses, he was washing or bathing he had great difficulty in finding the soap! Thinking to solve the problem, Mrs Douglas bought him a soap ball on a cotton rope which he could hang round his neck. He was delighted with it, and several days later he said to his wife, " It's wonderful—and look, it has hardly worn down at all."

Mrs Douglas looked at it. " No wonder," she said. " You haven't taken off the cellophane wrapping!"

HAVE you heard these anonymous lines concerning youth?

Youth is not a time of life—it is a state of mind. It is not a matter of ripe cheeks, red lips, and supple knees; it is a temper of the will, a quality of the imagination, a vigour of the emotions; it is a freshness of the deep springs of life.

Youth means a courage over timidity, of the appetite of adventure over love of ease. Nobody grows old merely by living a number of years.

Whether 17 or 70, there is in every being's heart the love of wonder, the sweet amazement at the stars and the starlike things and thoughts, the undaunted challenge of events, the unfailing child-like appetite for what's next, and the joy and the game of life.

PALS

A cat and dog existence
  Can be peaceful as can be,
And when both adore their master
  They are loving friends all three.

DAVID LIVINGSTONE wrote: " People talk of the sacrifice I have made by spending so much of my time in Africa . . . It is emphatically no sacrifice. Say, rather, it is a privilege."

The scope of any service we can give to others is likely to be much less than that of David Livingstone, but the fact is that when we love other people and try to help them, the idea of sacrifice never occurs to us—only that of joy and privilege.

A pity if we were to miss it!

IN one of his books Dr F. W. Boreham tells how, many years ago, he was strolling among the tulip beds in Rosherville Gardens, Gravesend. He was greatly impressed with the display of colour as he admired first one group of flowers and then another. Afterwards, leaving the gardens, he climbed a cliff path and looking down he saw the flower beds again, spread out beneath him.

But now he saw what he had not noticed as he walked among the flowers—they were all arranged in an elaborate pattern, and indeed across the centre some of the flowers formed letters which spelt out a motto. Before, he had been too close to see the full effect.

There are times when we need to try and distance ourselves a little from the things of everyday life if we are to see its full beauty. We let things " get on top of us ", as we say, and miss so much. A brief holiday, a change of scene and activity, perhaps even " forty winks ", can give that bit of perspective that we need.

We can be too close even to good and beautiful things.

THE FRIENDSHIP BOOK

A FRIEND who has just returned from a trip to Australia was very impressed by the fact that Australians always refer to the place where they live as " a home "—never " a house." Even estate agents use this term when they are conducting their business.

It reminded me of some words on a plaque which I once saw hanging over a fireplace:

The beauty of the home is order;
The blessing of the home is contentment;
The glory of the home is hospitality;
The crown of the home is Godliness.

That is how we make a house into a home.

HOSANNA; Blessed is he that cometh in the name of the Lord.

I WAS playing snakes and ladders with Roddy. He'd been off school with a sore throat and was finding convalescence a trial. He was also finding the game something of a trial for he was going down more snakes than he was going up ladders.

At last he burst out: " Mr Gay, wouldn't it be more fun if we went up the snakes?"

" Why not?" I said. " Go up the snakes and down the ladders."

Roddy thought for a minute and gave a big sigh.

" But I s'pose we'd need to have the downs as well as the ups, wouldn't we? There wouldn't be much fun if we didn't. P'raps we'd better just stick to the rules."

I see a bright future for Roddy!

THE FRIENDSHIP BOOK

THE Rev. George Duncan retired a few years ago after a lifetime's ministry in churches in Scotland and elsewhere. He once said that he had never forgotten a lesson he learned from a man called John Calder.

When Duncan was a very young man in Edinburgh, John Calder formed a handball team. George Duncan went along to join the team and Calder told him and the others that he had two rules that he wanted to make quite plain. The first was that he never intentionally *gave* offence—and the second was that he never *took* offence!

A wonderful example to follow.

I LIKE these one-verse poems written by Mrs Irene Winstone of Swansea. They say so much in a few lines:

It's easy to be nice, when everything's O.K.,
It's easy to be cheerful when you're having your own way,
But can you hold your head up and take it on the chin
When your heart is nearly breaking and you feel like giving in?

A millionaire with surplus cash, I know I'll never be,
But, with my dear ones by my side, this does not bother me.
I'm sure it's true for most of us small families everywhere—
We've all the riches that we need, if we have love to share.

BRITISH Prime Minister David Lloyd George was due to meet Eamon de Valera, Premier of the Irish Republic, for the first time. They were to meet at Downing Street in the wake of the Irish troubles of the time.

Lloyd George wondered how to approach the meeting. And then he decided. He had a Bible, a hymn-book, and a prayer-book placed upon the table. Mr de Valera sat on one side of the table and Mr Lloyd George on the other.

The Welshman asked the Irishman to say what Ireland wanted. He soon got his reply—they wanted this, that and the next thing. They were all political changes.

Lloyd George replied: " You are all wrong. You see these books. This is the Bible, this is a hymn-book and this is a prayer-book. These things, and not the things you are talking about, are the foundations of a people's greatness."

A FRIEND of ours who lived in a large house with a garden to match found both of them too much for him as he grew older so he moved into a small flat without a garden. When I visited him for the first time after his move I wasn't surprised to find seed trays and pot plants along the windowsill.

I noticed, too, a card which I presumed gave the names of the plants, but when I examined it I found it was a quotation copied from a writer whom I confess I had never heard of—Charles Dudley Warner.

It said, " To plant seeds and watch the renewal of life—this is the commonest delight of the race, the most satisfactory thing a man can do."

LISTEN . . .

Is there lovelier music,
Are there sweeter lays,
Than those the wind sings
And the sea plays?

E

SATURDAY—APRIL 21.

THIS is strictly between you and me, you understand, but did you hear about Mrs X. who stood in her kitchen, shaking her head and tut-tutting as she looked out at her neighbour's dingy, grey washing?

It wasn't until she stepped outside into her garden that she realised the washing on the next door line was perfectly clean. It was her own kitchen windows which were the trouble!

SUNDAY—APRIL 22.

BE not affrighted: Ye seek Jesus of Nazareth, which was crucified: he is risen; he is not here: behold the place where they laid him.

MONDAY—APRIL 23.

A HAPPY Easter to you! There are those who think that our word " Easter " comes from " Eostre ", the Anglo-Saxon goddess of spring, while some folklorists claim that it comes from an old word " *oster* " meaning " to rise."

It doesn't really matter. The rebirth of the countryside and the Resurrection of Jesus both have to do with newness of life.

Traditionally, people have worn new clothes at Easter as a symbol of this. A very old rhyme goes:

> *At Easter let your clothes be new,*
> *Or else be sure you it will rue.*

A rather more modern song says,

> *I could write a sonnet*
> *Upon your Easter bonnet!*

May Easter be a time of refreshment and renewal for us all.

THE FRIENDSHIP BOOK

DO you know the story of Sweetheart Abbey, in south-west Scotland? It was founded in the 13th century by John de Balliol and when he died in 1269, his widow, Lady Devorgilla, had his heart embalmed and placed in a small ivory casket which never left her side. On her death, it was interred beside her in her tomb in the Abbey.

Lady Devorgilla called it her " sweet heart and silent companion "—and that is how the word sweetheart is said to have been coined.

I REMEMBER the late Rev. Leslie Weatherhead, the well-known Methodist preacher, saying in a sermon " Even the ever-courteous BBC wrote to me once and said, ' When you are broadcasting, please do not *sing* near the microphone.' " Being a great singer, was not, Weatherhead frankly admitted, one of his gifts.

It reminded me of a verse I copied down many years ago:

" I've sung the Psalms of David for nearly eighty years,

They've been my staff and comfort and calmed life's many fears;

I'm sorry I disturb the choir, perhaps I'm doing wrong,

But when my heart is filled with praise I can't keep back a song."

Probably many of us have to choose carefully where we sing! But I am always glad if I hear someone humming or singing even if he or she is out of tune, because I think, " Here, truly, is a happy person!"

OLD ORDER

Our forebears had a way with stone
And left a glorious legacy;
Their very ruins seem to speak
Or order, prayer and piety.

THE FRIENDSHIP BOOK

FEW of us would claim to be theologians. Nor would Bruce Barton who wrote a book about Jesus called " The Man Nobody Knows ". In fact, his career was in advertising but he had a way of communicating religious truth in a way ordinary people could understand. For example, could anything be said more simply and more helpfully about God than this:

" God is supremely better than anyone has ever dared to believe. Not a petulant Creator who has lost control of His universe and in wrath was determined to destroy it all. Not a stern judge dispensing impersonal justice. Not a vain king who must be flattered and bribed into concessions of mercy. Not a rigid accountant checking up the sins against the penances and striking a cold hard balance. Not any of these. Nothing like these, but a Great Companion, a Loving Father."

WHEN the composer Ralph Vaughan Williams set about the task of editing the English Hymnal he wrote a tune for the hymn, " Come down, O Love Divine ". He called the tunc " Down Ampney ".

It was in the village of Down Ampney, in Gloucestershire, that Vaughan Williams was born in 1872. The peace of the English countryside and the pastoral scenes of his early childhood are reflected in this setting of the hymn which has remained a great favourite with choirs and congregations.

Once, when announcing this hymn, a clergyman told his congregation, " Look around this old church and you can *see* beauty; in this hymn you can *hear* beauty."

THE FRIENDSHIP BOOK

IN a television programme, the poet and author, Lawrence Durrell, was talking about the island of Rhodes where he lived for a number of years. Among the sights he showed us was a statue called the Marine Venus. Like many of these ancient statues she showed some of the ravages of the years, not least because, for some time, she lay at the bottom of the sea.

It is Durrell's comment I specially remember: " I like her for her imperfections—just in the same way that we like real people."

How true! None of us cares very much for " perfect " people. It is often their faults that endear them to us. And we can take some comfort from the fact that people probably like us for the same reason!

GO ye into all the world, and preach the gospel to every creature.

IN his autobiography, " In and Out of the Box," Robert Dougall, for many years one of television's best-known and best-loved newsreaders, says that of all the thousands of letters he has received from viewers he thinks his favourite is one from an old lady who explained that she was very deaf and liked to watch the news with her chair drawn up very close to her television set. However, she went on to say that if this put him off she would quite understand, and draw her chair further back!

Robert Dougall commented, " You couldn't have greater consideration than that!"

MAY

TUESDAY—MAY 1.

I WONDER whether you, like me, were ever puzzled by the title of the children's game, " Here we come gathering nuts in May?" Whoever heard of gathering nuts *in May?* But apparently, the song should be, " Here we come gathering *knots* in May," that is the knotted garlands of the May blossom and other flowers which played such an important part in ancient May Day ceremonies.

Many of our old May Day customs have been allowed to die out, but a mother with two small children at school tells me that last year the children in their class all made tiny May posies of flowers to take home to their mothers.

It occurs to me that we might bring some unexpected happiness to one or two people on this May Day if we took them a May garland.

WEDNESDAY—MAY 2.

HOW do you recognise Christianity? This is how I saw it described in a Plymouth church magazine:

In the home it is kindness; in business it is honesty; in society it is courtesy.

In work it is thoroughness; in play it is fairness.

Towards the fortunate it is congratulation.

Towards the unfortunate it is pity.

Towards the weak it is help; towards the wicked it is resistance.

Towards the strong it is trust; towards the penitent it is forgiveness.

Towards God it is reverence and love.

JEWELS

Set an artist to design
The perfect shape, the purest line,
Could he surpass, for all his skill,
What nature yearly does at will?

THE FRIENDSHIP BOOK

D R David J. Schwartz, an American academic and writer, tells in one of his books how proud his six-year-old son (also a David) was when he moved up from kindergarten.

" And what do you think you will be when you finish school?" asked Father.

" Dad, I want to be a Professor."

" A Professor? A Professor of what?"

David thought for a moment and then said, " I think I would like to be a Professor of Happiness!"

What a wonderful ambition! It's one we might all try to fulfil. No passing of examinations is needed.

D AG HAMMARSKJOLD was the second Secretary-General of the United Nations. In his eight-year tenure of the job he reached the stage where every member nation of the United Nations felt they could trust this bachelor Swede who exerted his own special patience and tactful influence as the world's chief peacemaker. He once commented that " your position never gives you the right to command—only the duty of so living that others can receive your orders without being humiliated."

Shortly before the plane taking him to mediate in the quarrel between Katanga and the central government of the Congo crashed, he recorded in his journal: " Pray that your loneliness may spur you into finding something to live for and great enough to die for."

Dag Hammarskjold had written his own obituary. He was posthumously awarded the Nobel Peace Prize for 1961—the only such prize to be awarded after the death of the recipient.

SATURDAY—MAY 5.

HAVE you heard of " Wonderful Walker "? He was Robert Walker and he was curate at Seathwaite in the Lake District for 67 years. William and Dorothy Wordsworth were two of his greatest friends and admirers.

Robert Walker did not write a book or a poem or achieve any financial success—indeed he lived in great poverty all his life. But people admired this " lowly, great and good man " because he loved and helped everybody around him, and enjoyed simple pleasures and a contented mind.

" Wonderful Walker's " good deeds are still remembered today.

SUNDAY—MAY 6.

THE Lord by wisdom hath founded the earth; by understanding hath he established the heavens.

MONDAY—MAY 7.

IN one of his books about prayer, the late Dr William Barclay says, " God has three answers to our prayers. Sometimes God says, ' Yes!' Sometimes God says ' No!' Sometimes God says, ' Wait!' "

Waiting is one of the things which many of us find hardest to do, yet if we can learn patience with our circumstances, patience with others, and perhaps most of all patience with ourselves, we are on the way to one of life's greatest secrets.

When I feel impatient and frustrated, I try to remember those great words of John Milton in his sonnet on his blindness, " They also serve who only stand and wait."

TUESDAY—MAY 8.

I CONFESS that, except in connection with the following quotation, I have never heard of Robert Jones Burdette who lived at the end of last century, but I shall always feel indebted to him for these words: " There are two days in the week upon which and about which I never worry. Two carefree days, kept sacredly free from fear and apprehension. One of these days is Yesterday, and the other is Tomorrow."

WEDNESDAY—MAY 9.

WE owe a lot to old Jonas Hanway. A social reformer, he co-operated with Robert Raikes in the Sunday School movement in England, and he also introduced us to the umbrella.

But he also had a " blind-spot "—" a bee in his bonnet "—about tea-drinking, especially in churches! He wrote, " In old times Ezekiel saw rivers of water rushing out from beneath the Temple. Today he would see rivers of tea! Next month will be the anniversary of the church. The ladies will be there with the tea pot. A member of the choir is to be married—out with the tea pot! The minister is leaving—where is the tea pot? Here comes the new minister—is the tea pot ready? The work party is about to begin a new season—hurry out the tea pot! Fie on you for a generation of tea-bibbers and guzzlers!"

Poor old Jonas Hanway! How little he understood! Someone came much nearer to the truth when he said that the cup of tea was the modern equivalent of the Biblical " cup of cold water given in the name of a disciple."

Long live the cuppa!

GIVE THANKS

Thank God for little villages
As well as mighty cities!
To lose those places, green and old,
Would be a thousand pities.

Good neighbours, quiet ways to walk,
  Sweet-scented country air—
These precious things belong by right
  To all who 'habit there.

THE FRIENDSHIP BOOK

THE late Professor T. H. Huxley once said that in the soil of England lie buried tropical seeds in great variety brought here by birds and the winds. He continued, " If for twelve months we could have in this country tropical heat we should be amazed by the coming out of strange seeds and our little gardens would bloom with tropical luxuriance."

That's what warmth could do—and I can't help thinking what hidden beauties can be revealed in the lives of other people by the warmth of our friendship and concern.

THERE must surely be only one village bus shelter in the country which has a railway station sign attached to its wall! It all happened because, years ago, Edward Thomas wrote a short poem, " Adlestrop " after his train had stopped briefly at the Gloucestershire village one summer afternoon.

> *The steam hissed. Someone cleared his throat,*
> *No-one left and no-one came,*
> *On the bare platform. What I saw*
> *Was Adlestrop—only the name.*

His verses brought fame to Adlestrop, so that when the station disappeared they put the station sign in the local bus shelter, with a plaque beneath bearing the poem.

Few of our fleeting memories are likely to bring that sort of result, but what they *can* bring is a deal of happy thought and reminiscence. How about sitting down quietly now and having five minutes of happy, fleeting memories of pleasant places, people and things?

A FRIEND of ours runs a business which makes great demands upon him day by day, but we are always amazed how he seems able to detach himself from the strain of it all. He certainly never brings his business troubles home with him.

He once confided to us that his secret lies in a little ritual which he learned from another businessman years ago. He always insists that his office calendar should be of the type that has a single tear-off date for each day. As he leaves the office he solemnly tears off the leaf, screws it into a ball, and drops it, almost ceremoniously, into the waste-paper basket. That day is finished with; tomorrow is another day. A philosophy, surely, that we might all do well to copy.

L ET thine heart retain my words: keep my commandments, and live.

A FRIEND occasionally sends us the Service paper of the church she attends. As well as the hymns and the Bible readings, it also has what is headed, " A Thought For The Week."

I am sure some of these will help you, as they have helped me:

" I do not know what the future holds, but I know who holds the future."

" You don't get much done by starting tomorrow."

" A smile has more than its face value."

" If you aim at nothing you hit it."

TUESDAY—MAY 15.

JUST recently I came across a book which described the beginning of war-time rationing in 1940. Do you remember the 4 oz. of tea, and 4 oz. of bacon, and the one and tuppence worth of meat? And then there was " snoek " and dried eggs—and all the wartime recipes, using substitutes like grated carrot in cakes and puddings.

And yet, as the writer of the book said, " Rationing, in some form, lasted for about 15 years yet it is said that the British people as a whole were never fitter nor better fed, for the diet, if sparse, was well-balanced."

Few, if any, of us would want to go back to the days of rationing, but there is a lot to be said for the simpler life. I think we might all take to heart the words used by Christian Aid: " Help us to live more simply, that others may simply live." And may we be thankful for small mercies.

WEDNESDAY—MAY 16.

I LIKE these lines entitled " A Happy Old Age " and pass them on:
A little more tired at the close of the day,
A little less anxious to have our own way.
A little less care for gain or gold;
A little more zest for the days of old.
A broader view and a saner mind;
A little more love for all mankind.
A little more love for the friends of youth,
A little more zeal for established truth.
A little more charity in our views,
A little less thirst for the latest news.
A little more leisure to sit and dream;
A little more real the things unseen.

THE FRIENDSHIP BOOK

WHEN you think about it, life consists of a multitude of simple acts of faith of one sort and another—planting bulbs in the garden, leaving the milk bottles on the step at night, posting a letter, putting our money in the bank, and so on.

Faith in ourselves, in our work, in other people, in God—this it is which gives meaning to life. It is faith, as somebody has said, which determines whether we spell life ' scared ' or ' sacred '.

THERE is surely something remarkable about a poet who is both blind and deaf; so much of his work would seem to depend on things seen and heard. The writer Ronald Charles Scriven went suddenly deaf at the age of 8 and gradually blind over the next 30 years.

But as his sight diminished, he says he looked and looked as hard as he could at the trees and fields, the flowers and birds of his beloved Yorkshire countryside, and at the busy streets and the lights of his native city of Leeds. He was determined that these things should stay in his mind's eye and find expression in his work through all the subsequent years—as indeed they did. No one reading his poetry would guess that the descriptive lines were written by a man who could no longer see.

Perhaps when we can see and hear it does not occur to us to " look and look " and so store our own minds with things of beauty; but how much richer we should be if we did, so that in quiet moments they would, as Wordsworth put it of his daffodils, " flash upon the inward eye ". Such memories are a perpetual enrichment.

F

SATURDAY—MAY 19.

FOR some time Bruce had been looking off-colour so when I met him recently I was pleased to see him looking fighting fit and I told him so.

He grinned. " I used to take my worries to bed," he said, " so I was sleeping badly. Then I heard of the experience of an American preacher, Dr Vincent Peale. His tailor had advised him to remove everything from his suit pockets at night. It would keep his suit in good shape."

Dr Peale tried it and it worked so he then thought, " If it works with my suit it might work with my mind, too." And it did!

" So now I do the same as Dr Peale," said Bruce. " At bed-time I empty my mind of all clutter—and I never have a poor night's sleep."

Frustrations, regrets, resentments, anxieties — these were the things that were keeping Bruce awake. Some of them will creep back into his mind during the day, but if he keeps on throwing them out every night, they might just stay away for good!

SUNDAY—MAY 20.

FOR I know that my redeemer liveth, and that he shall stand at the latter day upon the earth.

MONDAY—MAY 21.

DO you welcome advice? Or do you prefer to take your own counsel? Sometimes it depends on the way advice is given.

The poet, Samuel Taylor Coleridge, once remarked: " Advice is like snow; the softer it falls, the longer it dwells upon and the deeper it sinks into the mind ".

TUESDAY—MAY 22.

A VISITING minister arrived to preach in a very large church. A steward met him at the door and conducted him to the vestry. As they walked down the aisle the steward said, " I hope you won't mind me mentioning it, sir, but you will have to keep your voice well up when you speak. The agnostics in this church are something terrible!"

WEDNESDAY—MAY 23.

IN 1970, when the idyllic calm of the Caribbean island of Trinidad was threatened by unrest among unemployed and disadvantaged young people, two men, Father Gerard Pantin, a Trinidad-born priest, and a former international cricketer named Wesley Hall, went among them asking " How can we help you?"

Folk wanted someone to get things done, not simply talk and then disappear. So whatever suggestions were made were at once implemented: replacing broken beams; visiting a sick mother; finding jobs for people; helping a young man who had run foul of the law; coaching a football team; all these and much more important projects such as the new Vocational Centre for community development, or play-groups for children.

The work mushroomed, most of it of necessity done by volunteers—which gave rise to its name—SERVOL—Service Volunteers for All. For a full decade the love displayed by the pioneers of Servol has gained the trust and gratitude of local folk. Servol kept busy *doing*, rather than debating; *serving* and *building*, rather than assessing and researching; showing *compassion* and *courage* in a society where gratitude was never expected—and seldom shown.

NATURE'S ART

We may not all be artists
But we all can use our eyes
To appreciate the beauty
Of the world that round us lies.

A LITTLE while ago I was in church listening to a sermon on the text, " Give, and it shall be given unto you," in the course of which the minister said, " A closed hand cannot receive."

Those words have kept recurring to me since, not only in the way the minister used them, but because they have reminded me of so many other things a closed hand cannot do. It can't shake hands. It can't wave a friendly greeting—only shake a threatening fist. It can't pat a little child on the head. It can't be laid re-assuringly on the shoulder of someone who is discouraged. It can't turn over the pages of a book, or play a musical instrument. It can't scatter seed or pluck a flower.

Thank God for the joys that come to us through our own open hands and those of others.

FRIDAY—MAY 25.

I CAME across this saying of Oscar Wilde's the other day: " Education is an admirable thing, but it is well to remember from time to time that nothing that is worth knowing can be taught."

This can be compared with something that George Adam Smith stated many years earlier: " He who refuses to be taught, loses from life its charm and sacredness. Cease to learn, and you will in time starve your powers of obedience, and all the rest of those delicate faculties which in their union are worship and the very strength of spiritual faith."

Those two quotations need not conflict. It's a fact, isn't it, that we are all learning something from the day we are born until the day we die, at school, by observation, by reflection, and through experience of life.

SATURDAY—MAY 26.

ONCE when the scientist, Thomas Edison, and his assistant had conducted 1000 unsuccessful experiments and the assistant was showing signs of despair and frustration, Edison said quietly, " Never mind. We now know 1000 ways it *won't* work!"

That's worth remembering if sometimes we get discouraged and impatient when our plans don't work out as we would wish. Like Edison we must press on patiently and hopefully; the solution that *will* work is getting nearer all the time.

SUNDAY—MAY 27.

THERE is a friend that sticketh closer than a brother.

MONDAY—MAY 28.

SOME recent Christian Aid literature described various projects in India and other places to bring water to outlying villages where often there is no well. It quotes the answer of a young girl living in the southern part of the . Sudan to the question, " Where do you get your water?"

" Oh," she said, " I walk two hours every time and two hours back. I do this twice a day. It is for our family—my parents, grandmother and five brothers and sisters. There is no well in our village."

And all we have to do is to turn on the tap . . . How greatly sometimes we take for granted what we call " the common mercies of life," forgetting that, for many people in the world, they are " uncommon mercies."

Think of that little girl next time you turn on the tap . . .

TUESDAY—MAY 29.

"REMINISCENCES of a Student's Life" by Jane Harrison who died in the early years of this century is a book probably few have ever heard of nowadays, but it is worth remembering for its concluding words of wisdom to those who are growing old: "Old age, believe me, is a good and pleasant time. It is true that you are gently shouldered off the stage, but then you are given such a comfortable front stall as a spectator, and if you have really played your part, you are more than content to sit down and watch."

WEDNESDAY—MAY 30.

MANY stories are told about Anna Pavlova, the Russian ballerina, but this one is new to me. Once in Edinburgh when she had danced her most famous role "The Dying Swan" there was a momentary silence before the rapturous applause rang out. In that silence a refined voice in the audience proclaimed loudly, "She's awfully like Mrs Wishart!"

THURSDAY—MAY 31.

SOMETIMES at the bottom of the page of a magazine you will find a very short item which has obviously been put in to fill up a blank space on the page—indeed, the technical name for such an item *is* "a filler".

I often find more help in these "fillers" than in the whole page which has gone before! Here is such an example which I came across recently: "Live, love, learn, think, give, laugh, try. Can you pack better advice into seven words?"

JUNE

FRIDAY—JUNE 1.

MIRIAM EKER wrote those thoughtful lines which she calls " Needed ":

Sunny weather's very nice,
We'd like it every day,
But people shouldn't pull a face
When rain is on the way.
They look so very gloomy,
Their spirits are so low,
But rain is most important—
How would the gardens grow?
And if the sky was never grey,
It really wouldn't do!
How could we then appreciate
The sky of deepest blue?

SATURDAY—JUNE 2.

JUST recently I switched on the television set and found myself quite by chance in the middle of a programme for beginners in art. Now, I am no artist. The Lady of the House says that if I were to draw an elephant I would have to label it to make sure it was recognised!

But I found this programme fascinating, and though the tutor had much to say about colours and brushes and so on, he insisted that one rule above all others for the artist was, " Look! Look! Look!"

And what a good rule for life, too! How much we miss of beauty and goodness simply because we don't look hard enough and long enough. I still don't think I shall make an artist but I am determined to look and look and look, and so enrich my life in other ways.

THE FRIENDSHIP BOOK

L O, the winter is past, the rain is over and gone; the flowers appear on the earth; the time of the singing of birds is come . . .

A LITTLE girl was struggling gamely through her prayers, in spite of the fact that her younger brother was teasing her mercilessly.

At last she could stand it no longer. She heaved a sigh and said: " Please God—excuse me a moment while I kick our Willie."

A BAPTIST minister, the Rev. J. M. Wieland, once amused his congregation by telling them that, having attended a church in America with a congregation of 2000, he first thought what a great thrill it would be to be part of such a congregation regularly, and then began to see where there was another side to it.

If the church had the same characteristics as the average church here with, say, a congregation of 100 it would mean that 145 people would enter during the singing of the first hymn. Thirty would be singing the wrong lines and 150 would be singing out of tune. During the service 40 children would drop their hymn books, 23 their handkerchiefs and small coins to the value of £3.50. There would be 510 coughs, 618 blown noses, 27 violent sneezes and 9 cases of severe cramp. During the service $2\frac{1}{2}$ lb. of mints would be consumed, 59 persons would doze and 15 actually fall asleep!

Who said " big is beautiful "?

THE FRIENDSHIP BOOK

ONE warm summer evening, I was standing on a country railway station platform, with time to wait, and think, and ponder. Behind me in a small copse of trees the birds were singing merrily and just at that moment came a lovely breath of wind wafting over the wall the delicious smell of new-mown grass.

We sometimes complain about the cost of things, but while we still have the song of the birds, the smell of the cut grass, and gentle refreshing breezes, life is good.

THE name of Victor Gollancz is perhaps best known as the founder of an English publishing house, most of whose excellent novels bear distinctive yellow dust-jackets.

But there was nothing yellow about Victor Gollancz. He believed that miracles can be made to happen if the will to perform them is strong enough, and he fought passionately against cruelty in any and every form. He believed in respect and reverence for all life. The baby new-born, the prisoner condemned, the wasp upon the window-sill, the grub beneath the stone: all had their rights, and none must be denied.

In 1951 he founded an association, one of the aims of which was to persuade the Government to increase its quota of overseas aid. It fights poverty and injustice all over the world and helps the under-privileged who are striving for self-reliance, power and dignity.

Few of the thousands who have been helped by War on Want will ever have heard of Victor Gollancz. This would not have worried this compassionate man. For him it was the deed that counted.

FRIDAY—JUNE 8.

DO you remember 1981, The Year of the Disabled? That summer, a group of blind people were invited to one of the Buckingham Palace garden parties. Helping the Queen to entertain her guests was Lady Diana Spencer, a few days before she became the Princess of Wales.

Someone who was there saw her pause to chat to the blind visitors and then slip off her engagement ring so that they could handle what others were able to see.

A delightful gesture, typical of the Princess who so quickly won the hearts of us all.

SATURDAY—JUNE 9.

DR DAVID CAIRNS tells how once when he was a boy he was returning in the train with his father and mother from a seaside holiday. He had a fishing line with him which had become terribly tangled and which he was struggling unsuccessfully to unravel. His father watched him for some time in silence and then said, " Let me try, David."

In just a few minutes his father had straightened out the line.

Recalling this incident many years afterwards Dr Cairns said, " Neither of us, I daresay, had any idea that we were giving or getting a picture that would be with me at least all my days, to show how God deals with us His children, and how we should deal with Him."

SUNDAY—JUNE 10.

TO every thing there is a season, and a time to every purpose under the heaven.

MONDAY—JUNE 11.

THE other day I discovered this prayer composed by Robert Louis Stevenson:

" The day returns and brings us the petty round of irritating concerns and duties. Help us to play the man; help us to perform them with laughter and kind faces; let cheerfulness abound with industry. Give us to go blithely on our business all this day; bring us to our resting beds weary and content and undishonoured, and grant us in the end the gift of sleep."

TUESDAY—JUNE 12.

THIS anonymous set of verses appeared some time ago in a church magazine:

> *The more you give,*
> *The more you get.*
> *The more you laugh,*
> *The less you fret;*
> *The more you do*
> *Unselfishly,*
> *The more you live,*
> *Abundantly.*
> *The more of everything*
> *You share,*
> *The more you'll always*
> *Have to spare.*
> *The more you love,*
> *The more you'll find*
> *That life is good*
> *And friends are kind.*
> *For only what*
> *We give away,*
> *Enriches us*
> *From day to day.*

BLOW!

When dealing with inflation
All you need is lots of puff,
And when you're young and healthy
You will always have enough!

THE great painter, Sir Joshua Reynolds, once said, " I look only at the best pictures, for the bad ones spoil my eyes."

Well, I don't suppose he meant that quite literally, but what a lot of harm we can do ourselves, in every part of life, by being satisfied with second-best. To look always for the good and true and lovely about us is one of the secrets of happy, satisfying living.

VISITORS to the Malvern Hills area earlier this century may have met a gentleman-cyclist enjoying the exercise amid beautiful scenery. They may even have recognised him as Edward Elgar, the composer.

Tourists can now visit Elgar's birthplace at Broadheath, Worcester, where he was born on 2nd June, 1857, or go to see the memorial window in Worcester Cathedral based on Elgar's " Dream of Gerontius." This is one of Elgar's most famous works, but its first performance in Birmingham on 3rd October, 1900 was such a disaster that it almost caused the composer to despair of his musical career.

He and his wife both loved John Henry Newman's poem " The Dream of Gerontius ". A copy had been given to them as a wedding gift. Into its musical setting, Elgar brought all his faith, devotion and dedication. From January to August 1900, he worked, putting into it all his musical genius. Then came the bitter blow. The conductor died; his replacement did not care for " modern oratorios"; the chorus was disappointing. The whole thing was a failure, but, phoenix-like, Elgar overcame the blow and lived to become one of England's greatest composers.

THE FRIENDSHIP BOOK

A FRIEND who was a student of the late Dr Alexander J. Grieve, theological college principal, recalls how once, in a sermon class, the length of sermons was being discussed. Dr Grieve's advice was:

" Never mind if now and again people glance at their watches during your sermon. The time to worry is if someone holds his watch to his ear to see if it has stopped!"

IN her book *My Memories of Six Reigns,* Princess Marie Louise tells of a young woman whose social life brought her into contact with many famous political figures of the day. Knowing that she had recently met both William Gladstone and Benjamin Disraeli a friend asked her what impression these two great men made upon her.

She replied, " After I met Mr Gladstone, I left feeling that he was the cleverest man in England, but after meeting Mr Disraeli I felt that I was the cleverest woman in England!"

What a great and useful art it is to make other people feel important! We all have it in our power—listening to people instead of doing all the talking ourselves, asking them about *their* interests instead of simply expounding our own. This is the way to make people feel important—and the way to make friends.

CAST thy bread upon the waters: for thou shalt find it after many days.

I WONDER if, like me, you sometimes find that words which have been familiar to you all your life suddenly take on a new meaning? This happened to me recently as I listened to a sermon in church. The preacher quoted the familiar words from Genesis, " The evening and the morning were the first day," and then commented, " We might have expected it the other way round—' the morning and the evening were the first day.' That seems the natural order. But the Bible writer sees the movement from the darkness towards the light!"

If I forget everything else in the sermon I shall remember that. " Towards the light!" So many of us see things moving towards gloom and darkness. Hope and happiness come when we believe that things are moving towards the light.

TUESDAY—JUNE 19.

AREN'T trees wonderful? In the Garden of Gethsemane there is to this day an olive tree which has been there since the days of Jesus. An old country proverb declares that " to be a man, you must beget a son and plant a tree." I am told that, in all nature, only trees and tortoises live longer than people.

The trees that we admire are nearly all older than we are. They shield us from sun, rain, wind and frost and give us a bit of privacy, too, if necessary. There is something lovely about a tree in full bloom—yet trees are not only beautiful to behold, they also form an essential part of the biological balance of nature.

In his book " I Planted Trees ", Richard St. Barbe Baker reminds us that a tree is really the cheapest large-scale parasol we can have.

A FRIEND recently sent me the service sheet for the Sunday School Anniversary service at his church. At the top of the page were some words of the poet, Francis Thompson, which were particularly appropriate but which I think we might well take to heart at many another time too:

" Know you what it is to be a child? It is to be something very different from a man. It is to believe in love, to believe in loveliness, to believe in belief."

I HAVE heard of nations, cities, towns and villages having their own special celebrations of one kind and another but till just recently I had never heard of a single *street* having such a ceremony. It seems that every year at Midsummer, Church Street, Kidderminster, holds a Feast of Peace and Good Neighbourhood. It has its origin in a bequest by an unknown maiden lady in the 15th century, who left 40/- to the inhabitants of Church Street to provide " farthing loaves " for the people of the street and to enable the male inhabitants to meet to settle any differences. The Fund was augmented 200 years later by John Brecknell who left £150 to provide tuppenny plum cakes for the children and unmarried women in the street, and pipes and tobacco for the men to smoke a " pipe of peace " when the toast " Peace and Good Neighbourhood " was proposed.

Although Church Street has now become a business and professional part of the town, the custom is still carried on with a supper at St Mary's Parish Church, attended by the Mayor, and the distribution, in Church Street of the " farthing loaves and tuppenny plum cakes."

G

FRIDAY—JUNE 22.

A FRIEND of ours who frequently addresses church groups tells us that recently he went to a meeting where his talk was to be followed by a discussion. The chairman introduced him to the audience and then outlined the programme of the meeting by saying, " First, we will listen to Mr —, and then before the discussion we will all have a cup of tea to refresh us!"

SATURDAY—JUNE 23.

I KNEW that Midsummer Day was also the festival day of John the Baptist, but in their book " Here's the Year " Peter Watkins and Erica Hughes point out something I had never noticed before. They say that choosing Midsummer Day in honour of John the Baptist was a stroke of genius on the part of the Church.

John the Baptist had said of Jesus: " He must increase and I must decrease." After Midsummer Day, when John's birth is celebrated, the days begin to shorten, whereas after Christmas, the birth of Jesus, they start to lengthen—a splendid illustration of the text.

Perhaps this is why, in the Middle Ages, John the Baptist was regarded as the patron saint of " the common man "—a category in which most of us probably feel ourselves to come. Let us rejoice today that we ordinary folk have our part to play in the life of the world.

SUNDAY—JUNE 24.

WHAT therefore God hath joined together, let not man put asunder.

A N old lady I knew years ago used to amuse me by saying that when confronted with an uncomfortable situation, " I used my tack."

She meant her tact, of course, but though she had the name wrong, she had the right attitude.

Sympathy, perception and, above all, kindness are ingredients of " tact ". They oil the wheels of life.

There was once a meeting where a newcomer was rude to an elderly member of a committee. In his younger day, the old gentleman would have spiritedly retorted, but he had mellowed and although his committee friends realised how the attack had hurt him, he merely said: " Perhaps I may be allowed to make a comment. I am a little deaf and so do not always catch what is said about me." A confrontation was thus avoided.

A technician at a northern Hearing Aid firm, who was not deaf and so did not wear a hearing aid, had a rather amusing way of saying " My hearing aid is turned off," when an unkind or bitter remark was made to him. Another example of the value of tact.

TUESDAY—JUNE 26.

W ILLIAM MORTON was a young Australian Army captain who was killed in action in 1917.

In his diary these words were found: " He has achieved success who has lived well, laughed often, and loved much; who has gained the respect of intelligent men, and the love of little children; who has left the world better than he found it; who has never lacked appreciation of earth's beauty, or failed to express it; who has always looked for the best in others and given the best he had; whose life is an inspiration, whose memory a benediction."

LAKELAND IDYLL

Though country places, it is true,
Are lovely all the seasons through,

*The golden summer sun's caress
Imparts a special loveliness.*

SOMETIMES old familiar truths make a fresh impact on us when they are expressed in a new and striking way. I am sure we all realise that one of the best ways of overcoming our own griefs and troubles is to go out and do something for someone else in need. That truth took a new grip on me when I read the following words in a book by Dr. Stanley Jones, an American missionary to India: " When I dig a man out of trouble, the hole which is left is the grave where I bury my own sorrow."

THE end of Mrs Ralston's house is the finest wall for bouncing a ball against for miles around. The only trouble is that if the ball doesn't come straight back it probably lands among Mrs Ralston's roses. And fond of children as she is, there comes a time when even a woman as patient as Mrs Ralston is driven to speaking her mind.

" Why don't you take your ball to the park?" she demanded of three youngsters who had just snapped off a branch of an old favourite, ' Madame Butterfly.' " You'd be able to throw the ball a lot farther."

The three looked at her for a minute, then: " But there's not a wall in the park, Mrs Ralston."

Some days Mrs Ralston would have had no reply to that bit of logic, but today she said sweetly: " I'm sorry, but you'll just have to get used to playing without a wall."

I'm sure Mrs Ralston would make no claim to being a philosopher, but didn't she put her finger on one of the most important facts of life—the sooner we get round to accepting there are certain things we *can't* have, the happier we'll all be?

JACQUES OFFENBACH, the famous Parisian composer, was for many years haunted by a half-remembered waltz tune which he had heard as a boy. One day, when visiting Vienna, he saw an old man who had collapsed in the street, and took him to his hotel room to recover. The old man's name was Zimmer—and he turned out to be the composer of the waltz! Unfortunately he was too old and ill to remember the whole of the piece himself, so Offenbach had to leave Vienna disappointed.

A few weeks later, however, he received a parcel containing the manuscript of the waltz and a letter explaining how the old man had discovered it locked away amongst his treasures. He had written it as a young man for his beautiful fiancée, who had died tragically on the eve of their marriage. Would Offenbach like to keep it as a token of their friendship?

The composer was only too glad to do so, and he published the lovely " Zimmer's Waltz," which might otherwise have been lost for ever.

SATURDAY—JUNE 30.

A FARMER in the American Middle West read that in a neighbouring town there was a zoo where the keeper had trained a lion and a lamb to lie down peacefully side by side. The farmer visited the zoo next time he went to town, and indeed found the lion and the lamb lying beside one another. He asked the keeper if there was some trick about it.

" No," replied the keeper, " it's quite genuine, and has been going on for three months. But I don't mind telling you that there have been quite a few replacements!"

JULY

SUNDAY—JULY 1.

THE thing that hath been, it is that which shall be; and that which shall be done: and there is no new thing under the sun.

MONDAY—JULY 2.

I WAS told the other day about parents who took their small son of 18 months to have his photograph taken. The photographer sat Peter on a rug on the studio floor and tried to get him to smile, but he remained as solemn as an owl. All the photographer's efforts were in vain.

Mum and Dad tickled his toes and peeped at him from behind screens, but Peter only looked glummer and glummer. Suddenly he seemed about to burst into tears and his father ran to him, determined to avoid that at all costs. In his hurry he tripped over the edge of the carpet and fell on his back with his legs in the air. An easel which he had knocked over landed on top of him.

At once a great smile spread over Peter's face, and then he began to chuckle gleefully! The photographer clicked his camera and the result was a really lovely photo of a laughing child.

It's an amusing story, but it's a reminder, too, that happiness is not something that can be made to order. If we hunt for it then it is likely to evade us. Happiness comes when we forget about it and become absorbed in what we do—helping others, working hard, developing a skill. In none of them are we *looking* for happiness, but you can be sure that if it is there we shall find it.

THE FRIENDSHIP BOOK

A LADY once bemoaned to John Ruskin, the artist, that she had just bought a handkerchief of delicate and expensive material and almost immediately had accidentally ruined it with a blot of ink.

Ruskin asked if he might take the handkerchief and though the lady was rather surprised at this request she agreed. A few days later he returned it to her. Beginning with the blot he had drawn a design on the handkerchief so that, instead of being spoiled, it had been turned into a thing of beauty.

I read somewhere that often, when repairing clothes, the Chinese do not make a plain patch or darn but try to make it into some colourful design—a dragon, a flower, a sun or moon. What a helpful philosophy of life it is to try to make something lovely out of the drab, or the unfortunate! It really can be done if we try.

WEDNESDAY—JULY 4.

I READ somewhere of a primitive African tribe whose language only allowed them to count up to " one "; anything beyond that was " many!" In a way it is amusing because it means that we have one mouth and one nose but many ears!

But I like the idea of abundance which this primitive arithmetic encourages. We tend to think of having " only this " or " only that." What a difference it would make if we would " think abundance "— how much we have to be grateful for, how many blessings we enjoy, how great our inheritance in things of goodness, beauty, truth and love. How happy we shall be if, for us, anything beyond " one " is " many "!

H

THURSDAY—JULY 5.

A S children we all loved to have stories read or told to us and I imagine that few, if any of us, have grown out of the delight. Age has nothing to do with the enjoyment of stories. Sir Philip Sidney, the 16th century writer and soldier, spoke in one of his books of " a tale which holdeth children from their play and old men from the chimney corner."

But long before that, no doubt, people sat in the shadows round the flickering light of a camp fire listening to stories; nowadays we sit in the shadows round the television set, but the demand is much the same—" Tell us a story!"

How grateful we should be to those who provide us with adventure, romance, drama, humour and much besides, for our leisure hours. When next we open that engrossing book we are in the middle of reading, let's remember to say a silent, " Thank you!"

FRIDAY—JULY 6.

W HEN Stanley Baldwin was Prime Minister he was visited one day at Chequers by a friend who recounted his experiences in South-Eastern Europe — a story of plots and counter-plots, oppression and vice.

At the end of it both men sat for several moments in a silence of depression and horror. Then Baldwin pointed to a bowl of roses on his desk, and said to his friend, " Plunge your face into those roses and thank God."

This was not escapism. It was a recognition that lasting values such as beauty can give us a faith which helps us to combat the things of ugliness and violence and evil. Let us look for beauty today—and thank God.

A MISSIONARY once told an audience that there are 365 " Fear nots " in the Bible. This may be correct—I have never counted them, but I certainly agree with the advice.

Many famous people have confirmed that most of the things they worried about never happened.

Philip Toynbee, the well-known author, once wrote, " Fear is always the enemy; the deepest of all the roots of evil." While the comedy-actor, Bill Maynard, who had faced many drastic ups and downs in his life, confessed on the radio: " Fear at the back of worry is almost always not so much fear of what is happening, as of worry of what is going to happen."

SUNDAY—JULY 8.

H E that hath pity upon the poor lendeth unto the Lord.

MONDAY— JULY 9.

T HE poems of William Arthur Dunkerley (better-known to his readers as John Oxenham) have brought comfort and inspiration to thousands of people. Our friend Mary, who lives alone, loves them and has committed many of them to memory. Often, when the Lady of the House and I visit her she will quote a verse or two, and I copied down the one she recited to me the other day:

> *Art thou lonely, o my brother?*
> *Share thy little with another!*
> *Stretch a hand to one unfriended,*
> *And thy loneliness is ended.*

Knowing Mary, I realised she was reciting that from her heart. I hope we can too.

COME IN!

Castles can be stark and grim,
　　Cathedrals cold and dark,
Mansions can be rather grand
　　Standing in a park;
But little churches everywhere
Attract us with their friendly air.

A FRIEND and I were talking about the rush and tension of modern life and I quoted the words of Indra Devi who says in one of her books, " Modern man works in a hurry, eats in a hurry, even rests in a hurry."

My friend smiled, " I couldn't agree more," and he took a little notebook from his pocket and read out a number of sayings which he had collected over the years and to which he turns when he feels the tension building up. Here are just four:

The beginning of a prayer quoted by the late Dr W. E. Sangster: " Slow me down, Lord."

A Hindu wish: " May love and harmony be with us all—Peace—Peace—Peace."

From a poem by Bob Rennie: " Ev'ry man needs his place of COOL, of silence."

Sir Walter Raleigh: " Give me my scallop shell of quiet."

These may help us too in time of tension; better still, we can make our own collection.

WEDNESDAY—JULY 11.

WHAT is heroism? For many people the word suggests bravery in battle while others will think of daring rescues or great journeys accomplished in the teeth of terrible odds.

But there is another kind of heroism, too. It is practised all around us every minute of the day by ordinary, everyday folk. Someone once called it " the heroism of going on," and that's what it is—just carrying on, keeping the flag flying, living out one's life in the quiet assurance of faith. Those good souls who do that are heroes and heroines too—though they would never think so!

JACQUES TATI, the famous French actor and film producer, always loved children and young people and delighted in their appreciation of his work. " Often," he said, " some seven-year-old would send me a letter, and perhaps a drawing. Always in the corner of it would be the sun!"

What a marvellous expression that is of the child-like mind, and of what it means for us to " become as little children ". Our word-pictures of life, as we grow older, so often seem to have a cloud in the corner instead of the sun.

FRIDAY—JULY 13.

SOME years ago in the Western Australian city of Perth, young Leonard Kendall lost his job as a representative for a firm of wholesale chemists when the firm went out of business.

He had only a small amount of capital and a motor vehicle, so he rented a room, bought an old typewriter, and began as a wholesaler in pharmaceuticals. His chemist and other medical customers assured him of continued support, providing he could deliver the goods. Manufacturers and their agents agreed to allow reasonable credit terms—except one large distributor who was insisting on cash on delivery for all transactions. It made his venture impossible.

Leonard got down on his knees and prayed. Afterwards, walking down the street, he met the manager of the concern which had refused him credit. The man stopped him and said, " We are now willing to grant you sixty days' credit on all your purchases."

It was Archbishop William Temple who remarked that, when we pray, coincidences start to happen.

SATURDAY—JULY 14.

WHAT a pity that all that is known by most people about St Swithin is the saying that the weather today, dry or fine, will determine the weather for the next 40 days.

But he has many more claims to fame. He was a greatly loved Bishop of Winchester in the 9th century, a friend of the poor, a man of great piety and humility, a trusted advisor to some of the Wessex kings, possibly to King Alfred himself—who like Swithin has suffered from being connected mainly with a legend—that of burning the cakes!

Let's not worry if we don't capture the headlines. Far better to leave behind us an influence of humility, love and service. This was St Swithin's real memorial.

SUNDAY—JULY 15.

MANY waters cannot quench love, neither can the floods drown it.

MONDAY—JULY 16.

MANY years ago when he was in America at the famous Northfield Convention, the Biblical scholar Dr F. B. Meyer attracted great crowds year after year. Then another visitor came—Dr Campbell Morgan—who was even more popular, drawing the crowds away from Meyer.

The latter admitted to his friends that he found himself tempted to jealousy. " The only way I can conquer my feeling," he said, " is to pray for him daily, which I do."

A great scholar, a great preacher, yes—but an even greater *man*.

PHILIP is now five years old, and there are times when his mother and father wish he would be quiet. He is an incessant chatterbox. They have even offered to sponsor him for ten pence for every hour he doesn't speak—they know they are never in danger of having to pay up!

It reminds me of an observation I heard recently: " It takes us about four years to learn to speak—and the other three-score to learn not to."

WEDNESDAY—JULY 18.

THIS poem was sent to me by Dorothy Tenbeath of Tewkesbury, Gloucestershire. She tells me the writer's name has been lost. Perhaps so, but the message is still loud and clear:

Lord, help me live from day to day
In such a self-forgetful way,
That even when I kneel to pray,
My prayer shall be for " Others."

Help me in all the work I do
To ever be sincere and true,
And know, that all I do for You
Must needs be done for " Others."

And when my work on earth is done,
And my new work in Heaven's begun,
May I forget the crown I've won,
While thinking still of " Others."

" Others." Lord, yes, " Others!"
Let this my motto be.
Help me to live for others
That I may live for Thee.

THE FRIENDSHIP BOOK

I WAS amused recently at a lecture when the speaker mentioned something which he attributed to the 18th century, then quickly corrected himself, saying, " No. The 19th century. How time flies!"

How it does, indeed! Some people get anxious about this: " So much to do, so little time to do it," they complain. But others see it as an exciting challenge, as Rudyard Kipling did when he spoke of filling " the unforgiving minute with sixty seconds' worth of distance run." And it *will* be exciting to see how much of love and goodness and kindness we can cheerfully pack into this day.

IAN and Adrian have been friends for many years. They studied music together and graduated at the same time.

Ian became a church organist and loved his playing then he had a car accident and lost the use of his right arm. He went through a very dark period and when Adrian took over the church organ he would not go to hear him play.

Adrian knew how his friend was feeling. One day he took Ian to the church, sat him in a pew and proceeded to wrap his own right arm in a sling. He then started to play the organ very efficiently with his feet and his left hand. For the sake of his friend he had been practising for weeks with one hand to show him that his handicap *could* be overcome.

Ian took the hint. He mastered his disability, and is now the church organist again.

That's what the word friendship is all about, isn't it?

SATURDAY—JULY 21.

HOW often do you look up and see the beauty in front of you? It may be a lovely sunset, the varied shades of green in fields, trees and bushes, or a handsome building. Or it may be a different sort of beauty altogether.

There is a tale of an old cleaner scrubbing an Art Gallery floor in the days when knees, buckets and scrubbing brushes were the main tools of her trade.

" What a lot of lovely paintings you have here," a visitor declared looking up at the walls.

" Yes, I suppose so—if you have time to look up. I haven't," came the bleak retort.

It is the same idea as the verse about two men looking out through prison bars; one saw only mud, the other stars.

Even the Psalmist who knew nothing of the ugliness and bleakness of modern cities and the bustle of industrial areas, declared, " I will lift up mine eyes unto the hills from whence cometh my help."

Well, if there are no hills in your vicinity, try looking " up " or " out " for some beauty every day. It will make such a difference to your life.

SUNDAY—JULY 22.

BOAST not thyself of tomorrow; for thou knowest not what a day may bring forth.

MONDAY—JULY 23.

DID you hear about the minister who took as his theme " The pure milk of the Word "?

He had been preaching about 25 minutes when some of the congregation began to wish it was condensed . . .

THE FRIENDSHIP BOOK

IN his book *Plants with a Purpose*, Richard Mabey, the well-known naturalist, tells of a friend of his who has a balsam poplar in her garden. He says it is not a particularly attractive-looking tree, ". . . but every April as the leaves unfurl . . . a glorious incense fills the lanes round her cottage. In her second spring there, a neighbour called to thank her for the pleasure her tree had given the village."

How often the things which give *us* pleasure turn out to have a wider influence than we realise.

I LIKE these touching lines by Angie Langcaster which seem to me to express just how every child feels:

Mummy's very clever; she knows all there is to know.
She knows what I am thinking, though I'm sure it doesn't show.
She knows when I am naughty even when she isn't there,
She always seems to find out what I did, no matter where.
She seems to know just who pushed whom if anybody falls,
And when she isn't in the room I'm sure she sees through walls!
And yet I wouldn't change a thing—even if I could—
For Mummy also knows when I've been trying to be good,
And if I feel unhappy or I get into a muddle,
She seems to know exactly when I need a kiss and cuddle!

IF ONLY . . .

We all know charming places
Where lucky people stay
And where, if all our dreams came true,
We'd settle down some day.

A CANADIAN visitor to England was taken to an ancient parish church by his host and was greatly intrigued by the group of people waiting for friends under the shelter of the lychgate. " That's what I like about your church gates," he said. " They are not for keeping people out, but rather for inviting them in."

Well, he may not have got the original purpose of lychgates quite right (designed as they were for holding the first part of the burial service), but what a thought for churches and for us all, that gates and doors are not just for keeping people out but also for inviting them in!

I T was Oliver Goldsmith who once remarked:
" Our greatest glory consists, not in never falling—but in rising every time we fall."

N OWADAYS it seems to be only at weddings that gentlemen wear floral buttonholes in church, though it was once quite a common custom particularly in country districts. But one of our elders, Tom, a keen gardener, continues the custom and there are few Sundays in the year when he appears without his buttonhole.

One Sunday when I admired it he said, " Well, I love my garden, you know, I enjoy looking at it." Then he added, rather quaintly, " When I wear it, I share it!"

I have a feeling there is a parable there that goes beyond buttonholes!

SUNDAY—JULY 29.

HE taught them as one that had authority, and not as the scribes.

MONDAY—JULY 30.

FIDDLER JONES is the hero of a poem by the American poet, Edgar Lee Masters, who died in 1950. Jones was a happy man who spent his time making music for others, and he ended his life with 40 acres of land, a broken fiddle . . . and not a single regret!

Well, now, what had he to show for his life? Forty acres—a decent-sized field, perhaps, but not all that much. A broken fiddle is pretty worthless. But to have made a lot of people happy and to have died with not even one regret—how wonderful!

Real happiness doesn't depend on wealth or poverty, good times or bad. It comes through what we can do for others. Fiddler Jones knew that.

TUESDAY—JULY 31.

IT is said that one of Beethoven's great melodies was composed in Vienna while Napoleon was bombarding the city. Amid the din of shot and shell the deaf musician was conscious only of the inner harmony which was engrossing him.

Of course, in part, it was his physical disability which made Beethoven unaware of the tumult going on around him, yet it is true that if we are deeply engrossed in some activity, if we concentrate on things of goodness and truth and beauty then it is possible for us to exclude much that disturbs and annoys. This is not escapism—it is a way of personal, inner victory over outward circumstances.

AUGUST

WEDNESDAY—AUGUST 1.

THE famous Benjamin Franklin once said: " The best thing to give your enemy is forgiveness; to an opponent, tolerance; to a friend, your ear; to your child, good example; to your father, reverence; to your mother, conduct that will make her proud of you; to yourself, respect; to all, charity."

THURSDAY—AUGUST 2.

SOME years ago two clergymen were holidaying in the Welsh mountains. There they met a shepherd boy who had never been to school.

They taught him the 23rd Psalm, beginning, " The Lord is my Shepherd ", and as he recited the first five words, to help him memorise them, they suggested that each finger on his left hand represent a word—" Just grasp your fingers one by one with your right hand as you say the words ' The Lord is my Shepherd '," they told him.

Next year they came upon a cottage in the same area. There they saw a photograph which they recognised as being the shepherd boy and enquired about him.

The woman who owned the cottage was the boy's mother. She said that the boy was dead. During the winter he had been looking after his sheep during a storm and had fallen over a precipice and died.

The clergyman told the boy's mother how they had met her son and what they had taught him.

" That explains something we never understood," she told them. When the boy had been found he had been grasping the last finger of his left hand.

FRIDAY—AUGUST 3.

THE pianist Arthur Rubinstein once took part in a radio quiz programme in which a record was played and he was asked if he could recognise the pianist.

He listened carefully and was obviously puzzled. " It sounds like my playing," he said, " but there aren't any wrong notes." He meant it, too, for he confesses to playing wrong notes even though many of us might not notice. Still, I think it is quite a comfort to know that even the great are not perfect—and more than that, that some of them are great enough to admit it.

SATURDAY—AUGUST 4.

ONE of the most famous and popular books of last century was " Self-help " by the Scottish writer, Dr. Samuel Smiles. The fascinating parts of the book are those in which he tells the true stories of people who had to try, try and try again before they achieved the results they were aiming at—such as the French potter, Bernard Palissy, who spent 16 apparently fruitless years until he finally mastered the art of enamelling earthenware.

Smiles himself writes: " We learn wisdom much more often from failure than from success. We often discover what *will* do, by finding out what will not do; and probably he who never made a mistake never made a discovery."

SUNDAY—AUGUST 5.

ONE generation passeth away, and another generation cometh: but the earth abideth for ever.

GREEN THOUGHTS

There still are quiet places
From cities far away,
Where, in leafy corners,
Beauty holds its sway.
There nature whispers to the heart
Truths only she can e'er impart.

MONDAY—AUGUST 6.

MUCH of our enjoyment of life comes through our five senses of tasting, touching, smelling, seeing and hearing. Dr Magnus Pyke, whose books and television programmes have fascinated thousands of people, says that all our senses are involved in our enjoyment of food—and if you wonder, as I did, about where hearing comes into it—he continued: " Who would enjoy eating silent celery?"

A minor point, perhaps, yet I wonder whether we don't all miss a great deal in life because we haven't cultivated our senses as greatly as we ought. People walk in the country and yet miss the sights and sounds that delight the trained eye and ear.

Suppose that, just for a week, we make a point of trying to be specially aware of just one thing to gladden each of our five senses in turn. I think it would turn out to be a rather wonderful week.

TUESDAY—AUGUST 7.

MANY of us must have read with delight at least some of the books of the Yorkshire vet, James Herriot, who wrote " All Creatures Great and Small ", " It Shouldn't Happen to a Vet", " Let Sleeping Vets Lie " and so on.

The idea of writing came to him when on his rounds he listened to a short story on his car radio. He felt he could do better himself. At first it did not prove so easy. Story after story was rejected. But the encouragement of his wife Helen made him persist in his efforts till he became the best-selling writer we know today.

Our efforts and *others'* encouragement—what a large part these things play in our lives, even if we never write a best-seller!

ONE of the greatly-loved bishops of last century was Dr William Walsham How whose last appointment was as Bishop of Wakefield from 1888-1897. To him we owe such well-known hymns as " For all the saints who from their labours rest ", " It is a thing most wonderful ", " Summer suns are glowing " and many others.

But it was perhaps his work in the East End of London for which he is best remembered. Although coming from a wealthy background, he lived a life of sacrificial service, closely identifying himself with his poor parishioners. Indeed, because he scorned the private coach he could have used and travelled by public transport he won for himself the title, " The Omnibus Bishop "! Truly a " Prince of the Church ", who never lost " the common touch ".

IN his famous book, " The Compleat Angler," Izaak Walton has a passage in which he describes the beauty of the woods and meadows in which he wandered, and the sparkling streams where he fished and admits that all this belonged to someone else, with all the responsibilities of ownership, though he (Izaak) has the full and free enjoyment of it. He speaks of sitting on the river bank " joying in my own happy condition and pitying this poor, rich man that owned this and many other pleasant groves and meadows about me."

This is not to suggest we should expect " everything for nothing," but it is a reminder to us of how much goodness and gladness there is in life which comes to us at the hands of others. No man is an island.

A UTOGRAPH albums may seem a little out of date these days but they are often interesting and amusing to browse through. I came across the following recently in a friend's book which he had unearthed from a box in his attic:

> *'Twixt the optimist and the pessimist*
> *The difference is droll:*
> *The optimist sees the doughnut*
> *While the pessimist sees the hole!*

A familiar truth expressed in a rather different way!

SATURDAY—AUGUST 11.

W E only have to look around our own homes, let alone the larger world about us, to realise how greatly our lives have been enriched and our labour eased by inventions of one kind or another. Perhaps it would be worth while to make a list of the things we did not have, say twenty years ago. And I sometimes wonder what incredible things may be invented in the next twenty years!

But it is worth remembering the words of a character in Noel Coward's play " Design for Living " who complains that amid all the inventions of this 20th century no-one has yet invented anything " to create quiet and calm ".

No, some things are far beyond the skills and techniques of man to create—and always will be. A humbling thought.

SUNDAY—AUGUST 12.

W HERE there is no vision, the people perish: but he that keepeth the law, happy is he.

STEPPING OUT

A day in the country,
A tale to be told,
Memories to cherish
When he is old.

MONDAY—AUGUST 13.

THE other day the Lady of the House and I had to make a visit which could not be delayed, though if possible we would like to have postponed it because it was pouring rain. However, clad in macs and armed with umbrellas we braved the elements, feeling, I must confess, none too cheerful.

Nor were our spirits improved by a friend we met on the corner who moaned, " This is terrible, isn't it?" Fifty yards on, we almost collided with another friend who shook the raindrops from his chin and said, with a cheerful smile, " this will do the garden good!"

What a difference *his* words made to our spirits! I was reminded of the words of an anonymous writer: " When we travel we change our skies but not our minds!" We can't control the weather, or, indeed, many of our circumstances, but we can control our thoughts about these things.

TUESDAY—AUGUST 14.

A SCHOLAR in China was translating part of the New Testament into a local dialect and found himself stuck because he could not find an appropriate word or phrase for " Comforter." He left the passage for a while and went on to other work and then it so happened that one of his native workers came to ask for a few days off.

He explained that his sister had lost her little baby and was in great distress. " I would like to go to her," he said, " so that I can help her heart to get round the corner." The translator's problem was solved! There was the phrase he needed. I wonder if, today, there is someone whose heart *we* can " help round the corner "?

I WAS impressed by some words of Lord Norwich written after a visit to the famous Pyramids of Egypt.

He was saddened that so many visitors treated the pyramids with scant respect, staying only long enough to get themselves photographed.

" The only way to get the full impact of the Pyramids," he writes, " is to spend the night in the local hotel. Walk to them at sunset when the last tourist buses have gone; go again after dinner; go a third time—and best of all—at dawn. Gradually, by these repeated visits the miracle unfolds and the magnitude of the achievement of those early Pharoahs sinks in."

How much we miss in life because we are in too much of a hurry. We see things, but we never really *look* at them. Yet there is so much that only really yields up its wonder when we look, and look, and look again!

NOWADAYS, with our scientifically accurate watches and quartz clocks, few of us, except in a moment of idle curiosity, try to use a sundial to tell the time. However, if you are like me you are probably intrigued by the wit and wisdom which sometimes appears in the inscriptions on these ancient time-pieces.

Tempus fugit, for example, appears over and over again, but occasionally one comes upon an unfamiliar one such as this, which I saw recently:

Shadow and sun—so too our lives are made—
Here learn how great the sun, how small the shade!
Wisdom indeed.

I ENVY the knack most women have of being able to nurture and sustain a close friendship which often lasts as long as life itself.

The Lady of the House is fortunate in sharing such a powerful bond with her old school friend, Daphne. We don't see her very often because distance prevents it, but her regular letters are always a joy. When things go well for us she rejoices. When things go wrong she is genuinely concerned and does her best to cheer us up. I know she also mentions us in her prayers from time to time.

One Monday morning when Daphne's welcome letter plopped through our letter box, my wife took one look at the familiar scribble and said, beaming, " Look Francis, what a lovely start to the week!"

I was reminded then of the words of the poet, Shelley, who said, " Friendship, a dear balm—whose coming is as light and music are."

SATURDAY—AUGUST 18.

I LIKE the little story of four-year-old Hannah, whose parents had been trying to teach her good manners. She came dashing in from play one day and said, " Mummy, can I have a banana?"

Her mother wagged a finger and said, " What's the magic word?"

Hannah momentarily paused, and then said, " Is it abracadabra?"

SUNDAY—AUGUST 19.

WHOSOEVER shall receive one of such children in my name, receiveth me: and whosoever shall receive me, receiveth not me, but him that sent me.

JUST LOOK!

There are wonders all around us,
    Every minute, every day,
But only children see them
    For they find them in their play.

IF we were asked to choose our favourite colour not many of us would name grey. It's considered to be a rather dull colour.

Yet I remember a passage in one of G.K. Chesterton's essays in which he puts grey in a very different light. He talks of the variety of greys—the grey of steel, or the grey of the plumage of a dove. He takes delight in the grey that can mingle with red in the morning clouds. He sees beauty and variety even in grey hairs.

And how right he is! Beauty is in the eye of the beholder. I think we could all add to Chesterton's list if we went about today looking for " the beauty of grey ".

FRANK LOESSER, the American song-writer, was responsible for the immensely popular musicals " Guys and Dolls," " Where's Charlie?" and " Most Happy Fella."

Once, in an interview, he was asked where he got his ideas for his songs and replied, " Oh, they just pop into my head!" Then he added, " Of course, your head has to be arranged to receive them. Some people's heads are arranged so that they keep getting colds. I keep getting songs!"

Well, I don't suppose it was as easy as all that, but " a head that is arranged "—or perhaps we ought to say rather, " a heart that is attuned " to certain things does seem to attract those things to itself. Gloomy thoughts attract more of the same kind, but a heart attuned to beauty, goodness, kindness and happiness acts as a kind of magnet—just as if those things were always " popping into our heads ".

FRANCIS DE SALES, the early 17th-century Bishop of Geneva, won fame in the Church through his reform and re-organisation of this very difficult diocese, and through his voluminous writings. But neither of these demanding jobs led him to neglect his preaching and his pastoral work. He used to say, " Whoever preaches in love preaches effectively."

His friends sometimes remonstrated with him about the way he allowed people to consume his precious time about comparative trifles. " But these things are important to those whom they concern," was his reply, " and the persons in question want help as much as others."

If a man as great and as busy as Francis de Sales could find time to listen to the concerns of others, we, too, should have time.

NOT far from Windsor Castle, the village blacksmith of Salt Hill used to read aloud every evening by the light of his forge after his day's work was over.

Most of his neighbours could not read, so they gathered round him to listen to a story. On one occasion it was a collection of letters written by the novelist Samuel Richardson and entitled " Pamela."

The neighbours became more and more interested, and when, after many readings, the story ended, and hero and heroine were united in the bonds of holy wedlock, the simple villagers were so delighted that they rushed to the little village church on the outskirts of Slough, and rang a merry peal of bells in honour of the wedding!

FRIDAY—AUGUST 24.

JAMES McNEIL WHISTLER, the 19th century American artist, once received a complaint from a purchaser about the price of a painting. The man said to him, " For two days' labour you ask 200 guineas!"

" No," replied Whistler quietly. " I ask it for the knowledge of a lifetime."

There is a truth here about more than pictures. I wonder if we ever stop to think about the skill and knowledge and experience which have gone into many of the things we buy or possess—even the most ordinary goods and services? We are all debtors to a greater extent than we realise.

SATURDAY—AUGUST 25.

A MISSIONARY has told how he was once lost when travelling in Africa. At last he met a native who undertook to guide him home through the trackless jungle. After some time the missionary became uneasy as to whether they were going in the right direction.

" Are you sure this is the right way?" he asked his guide.

" There is no way," was the reply. " I am the way."

What an important element in our life trust is! And how fortunate we are if we have friends and loved ones whom we can trust implicitly however dark and long the way.

SUNDAY—AUGUST 26.

IF any man desire to be first, the same shall be last of all, and servant of all.

BREEZE OF MORNING

THE FRIENDSHIP BOOK

I DON'T remember the days when sermons were timed by an hour glass on the pulpit, but I do recall thinking as a small boy, that what we called the " long prayer " seemed to go on for hours!

The late Dr W. E. Sangster, the well-known Methodist preacher, used to speak of what he called " minute prayers "—brief prayers " shot out," as he put it, at any moment of the day, in a way that can keep us in constant touch with the sense of God's presence. There could be a lot of prayer in a few words, he suggested.

We may well find that some of our most meaningful prayers are of that kind—a verse of a hymn, a sentence of scripture, a simple request, or confession, or thanksgiving. As someone has said, " God gave us two ears but only one mouth, therefore we ought to listen much, and speak little."

D ANCING, in one form or another, seems to be as old as mankind. I confess I am not much of a dancer (as the Lady of the House—or, at least her feet, would testify!) I am rather like the man in P.G. Wodehouse's story: " The Man with the Two Left Feet "!

But a passage I came across by an anonymous writer the other day reminded me that we all ought to be dancers in some way whether we do it with our feet or not. He described the importance of " ... dancing with the feet, with ideas, with words, and, need I also add, that one must also be able to dance with the pen." A plea indeed, for liveliness, for gaiety in all we do. Of *that* sort of dancing I *can* approve.

THE FRIENDSHIP BOOK

AN American writer, Danny Thomas, said that the best advice about life he ever received was from his mother who said, " Never carry yesterday about upon your back. If you do you will be bent double by the time you're 21!"

Perhaps that doesn't sound much comfort to those of us who are over 21! But it is never too late to shake the burden off, stand upright and start all over again.

WE don't often think of nicknames in connection with the Bible, but there are certainly some there—James and John, for example, whom Jesus called " the sons of thunder ".

Then there is Barnabas in the Book of Acts. His real name was Joses (or Joseph) but he was called Barnabas which meant " one who encourages ".

What a splendid nickname to earn for oneself! I think most of us would be glad to think we could earn it—and why shouldn't we? It just needs a little sympathy and cheerfulness to lift people up instead of slapping them down.

PROBABLY all of us who belong to the Christian church have periods of discouragement and frustration when we look out on a world which often seems to pay scant regard to the things in which we believe. Whenever I feel like that I recall the story of a young woman who complained to her minister, " It's so difficult to be a Christian in modern times."

" But, my dear," he replied gently, " Christians have *always* had to live in modern times!"

GOLDEN HOURS

Sweet are the ways of Autumn
As Summer's lease expires
And trees begin to shed their leaves
To burn in glowing fires.

SEPTEMBER

SATURDAY—SEPTEMBER 1.

A CCORDING to legend, there was once an abbey which had a very generous abbot. No beggar was ever turned away and he gave all he could to the needy. The strange thing was that the more he gave away the richer the abbey seemed to become.

When the old abbot died, he was replaced by a new one with exactly the opposite nature—he was mean and niggardly.

One day an elderly man arrived at the monastery saying that he had stayed there years before, and was seeking shelter again. The abbot was busily engaged elsewhere so the door-keeper took pity on the visitor and found a cell for him. He apologised for the meagre hospitality they could offer saying, " Our monastery cannot provide for strangers like it used to when we were wealthy. No-one seems to make gifts towards our work nowadays."

" Ah, well," said the stranger, " I think that is because you banished two brothers from the monastery."

" I don't think we ever did that," said the puzzled door-keeper.

" Oh, yes," was the reply. " They were twins. One was called ' Give ' and the other,' It shall be given unto you.' You banished ' Give ', so his brother decided to go as well."

SUNDAY—SEPTEMBER 2.

H E arose, and rebuked the wind, and said unto the sea, Peace, be still. And the wind ceased, and there was a great calm.

K

MONDAY—SEPTEMBER 3.

IT was Henry Wadsworth Longfellow who wrote the well-known verse:

> *Lives of great men all remind us*
> *We can make our lives sublime,*
> *And, departing, leave behind us*
> *Footprints on the sands of time.*

But I wonder how many folk remember the following lines which make the previous verse even more full of meaning:

> *Footprints, that perhaps another,*
> *Sailing o'er life's solemn main,*
> *A forlorn and ship-wrecked brother,*
> *Seeing, shall take heart again.*

These words remind us that if we can see that someone else has trod the way before us, it gives us encouragement to follow.

TUESDAY—SEPTEMBER 4.

SHOULD we celebrate a National Grandparents Day?

They have done so in the United States of America since Congress in 1979 fixed one on the first Sunday in September.

The President of the time, Jimmy Carter, said at the time: " Grandparents are our continuing tie to the near past, to the events and beliefs and experiences that so strongly affect our lives and the world around us. We all know grandparents whose values transcend passing fads and pressures, and who possess the wisdom of distilled pain and joy. Because they are usually free to love and guide and befriend the young without having to take daily responsibility for them, they can often reach out past pride and fear of failure and close the space between generations."

THE FRIENDSHIP BOOK

I LOOKED out of the window the other day and noticed a tree standing forlornly on the horizon. Nearer home I noticed a plant in the garden that didn't seem to have much life in it.

It made me stop and think. Do we judge the beauty of a landscape by a single tree? Dislike a garden because of one faded flower or lifeless plant? I'm sure we don't—and yet if we are in a critical mood, we can so easily let the flaws influence our feeling towards the countryside, a garden, a town—even our friends.

None of us is perfect. We all have our flaws. Let's make a vow to overlook them in others, and always to search out the best.

OUR friend Thomas is a keen gardener and it is always a great joy to walk round his garden. Recently, I was admiring some beautiful double chrysanthemums he had on show.

" Yes, they're fine," he agreed, but seemed to hesitate as he said it. I looked at him questioningly, and waited for him to continue. " Yes, there have been some wonderful developments—new varieties and all the rest of it. Yet sometimes, you know, I think we brush aside too easily the simple types, the single flowers with their delicate perfection." And he led me across the lawn and pointed out to me just such an example.

No-one, I think, would want to lose some of the wonderful developments which man's skill and care has brought to all kinds of things, but I think we need to remember Rudyard Kipling's prayer, " Teach us delight in simple things . . . "

A CHURCH magazine's request for children's sayings brought this delightful story from a lady in Coventry.

Her grandson, Kevin, about seven years old, had persuaded her to play football with him in the garden.

" More by luck than good management, I scored a goal. Kevin came running up to me and flung his arms around me, saying, ' And now we've got to love each other '!"

SATURDAY—SEPTEMBER 8.

WHEN we were on holiday, the Lady of the House and I visited Widecombe in Devon and there we made two interesting discoveries. The first was that the famous Widecombe Fair was not one of the really ancient fairs dating back (as some of them do) to the Middle Ages, but that it began as comparatively recently as 1850.

The other discovery was that the great granite church tower built about 1500 was paid for by the local tin miners, who, as Garry Hogg has written, " had found unexpected prosperity; like the wool merchants of Suffolk and the Cotswolds, they paid tribute to the God who had favoured them."

As we sat quietly in this magnificent church, known locally as the Cathedral of the Moor, we remembered how great and humble alike have played their parts in our spiritual heritage and we paid *our* tribute of thanks to God, too.

SUNDAY—SEPTEMBER 9.

THEY that are whole have no need of the physician, but they that are sick.

THE FRIENDSHIP BOOK

I COULDN'T help smiling when somebody said rather cynically, " Never put off till tomorrow what you should have done in the early nineteen-seventies!"

Well, I hope we are not as bad as that, but I imagine that most of us, at some time or other, are guilty of what we call procrastination—that letter we really must answer, the borrowed book we are going to return, a call we have promised ourselves to make.

I am sure we could make someone happy today if we did just *one* of those things we have been putting off for some time. Well, how about it?

THE grounds, as well as the buildings themselves, of many of our stately homes attract thousands of visitors every year. Blenheim, Chatsworth, Croome, Burleigh, Broadlands, Warwick Castle and Stowe all have in common the fact that their grounds were landscaped by " Capability Brown "—one of the most famous landscape gardeners of all time.

His genius lay in his gift of transforming the formal flower beds and clipped hedges into vistas of natural scenic splendour. Christened Lancelot, his name " Capability " was given to him because of his habit of saying, when surveying a site to be landscaped, that it was " capable "—capable, that is, of being transformed into one of his imaginative schemes.

How much more exciting life could become for most of us if we saw it in terms of " capability ", of what it might be, instead of just accepting it as it is. Imagination is one of God's gifts to us for enlarging and improving our lives.

WEDNESDAY—SEPTEMBER 12.

IN one of her books Rita Snowden tells the delightful story of two young Dutch visitors who were staying with her and who were having difficulty with the English language.

They had spent the morning looking round the village and its shops and came back with a vase which had taken their fancy. " We haf it from the house of two hans," they told her.

Not surprisingly, Rita Snowden was puzzled. " From *where*?" she asked.

" From the house of two hans," they repeated.

It was some time before it dawned on her that they meant the second-hand shop!

THURSDAY—SEPTEMBER 13.

IN September, 1981, the 8th Earl Nelson died at his Norfolk home at the age of 76. Earlier that year he had been walking across Trafalgar Square in London, talking to Miss Christina Foyle, owner of the famous bookshop, when he was stopped by an American tourist who asked to be directed to " the famous Foyle's bookshop."

" Go up there past the lights, and you'll come to it about a quarter of a mile along on the left," Lord Nelson told him. " And it might interest you to know that my companion here is actually Christina Foyle herself."

The coincidence seemed too much for the American. Jerking his thumb up towards the figure on the tall pillar in the Square, he remarked sardonically: " And I guess you'll be telling me next that you're Lord Nelson."

" Well," replied the Earl, " as a matter of fact I am."

THE FRIENDSHIP BOOK

A GROUP of local churches carried out a project called " Outreach " which consisted of a house-to-house visitation throughout the parish. Asked afterwards if she thought the campaign had done any good, one of the visitors replied, " Well, if you mean in terms of bringing many people to church, I just don't know; but it has done *me* good." She explained that it had helped her to overcome her shyness when speaking to strangers and won her new friends.

How true it is that when we engage in some sort of enterprise for others we are ourselves enriched through it. " Give, and you shall receive."

I WAS listening to a radio programme about the annual Chelsea Flower Show. The remark of one commentator struck me forcibly when he came to a water garden. He said, " You know, a water garden has everything—colour, movement and sound. There is a kind of bonus here even to the usual beauty of a garden."

We may not have a water garden ourselves but maybe we have access to one in a local park—or the countryside will supply it. When I mentioned this colour, movement and sound to a friend, he said, " Well, Francis, we can find these things in a busy city, too, if we look for them. Colour, movement and sound are everwhere about us."

" He's right you know!

I CAME not to call the righteous, but sinners to repentance.

A HAPPY PLACE

The world is full of beauty spots
Where tourists like to go
But there are quiet corners still
Which many do not know.
There Nature wears a smiling face
And Man has added warmth and grace.

I HAVE just been re-reading one of H. V. Morton's famous travel books " In Search of Ireland " which tells of the tour he made there over fifty years ago.

One evening he found himself the sole visitor to a monastery at Melleray but a lay-brother offered to conduct him round, explaining the various parts of the building and the way of life of its inhabitants.

Then, as they parted at the gates of the monastery the lay-brother said, " Pray for me tonight and I will pray for you. If all the world did that how different it might be."

TUESDAY—SEPTEMBER 18.

IT was the 100th anniversary of the Sunday School and after the service there was a reunion tea at which a number of " old boys " and " old girls " had been invited to give brief reminiscences of their Sunday School days.

One of the speakers had enjoyed a particularly distinguished career, but he astonished his hearers with the simplicity of his testimony. " There was one lesson which has had more influence on my life than anything else I can think of," he said. " The teacher had been talking about the joy of Jesus and at the end of the lesson she had said, ' I want you each to do three things every day this coming week. I want you to learn something lovely by heart—a sentence of scripture or a verse of a hymn; I want you to look for something lovely; and I want you to do something kind and helpful for someone. Then *you* will be happy.' "

The speaker paused and then he said quietly, " It worked—and it still works."

DO you ever find difficulty in going to sleep? I heard of one little boy who didn't know how to say his prayers, or what to say to God, so he just went through the alphabet and then said: " Dear God, you put the letters into words and make them into a prayer."

Some time ago, when I was in a strange bed and finding it difficult to drop asleep, I thought back to that small boy and began to use the alphabet to pray. For each letter of the alphabet I remembered before God one person whose name began with that letter—and I certainly hadn't gone right through the full twenty-six before I had fallen asleep.

I don't, of course, regard this as a substitute for normal daily devotions, but after all, it helps others when we pray for them—and if it helps us to get to sleep, too, then it's no bad thing, is it?

I REMEMBER watching some archaeologists at work patiently scraping away the soil in the foundations of an ancient building. There is a sense of adventure and excitement in a project like this — quieter, perhaps, than in undertakings to which we usually apply those words, but every bit as real.

A now familiar but still very moving example must have been when Dr Arthur Hunt, exploring the ruins of a city by the Nile, came upon a scrap of papyrus containing these words attributed to Jesus but not in the Bible: " Raise the stone, and thou shalt find me; cleave the wood and there am I."

Joy in work, glory in the commonplace—these are discoveries we can all make, as exciting as those of any archaeologist.

A MAGISTRATE in a juvenile court was reading a report in which it said that a boy liked swimming and canoeing.

The magistrate commented: " Good, he likes water."

In a very audible whisper, the boy's mother was heard to say, " Yes, but not when it comes to washing his neck!"

OUR old friend Mary lives right opposite the church in which she was baptised and married. She saw her children brought up there and her husband lies buried in the churchyard.

She attended its services regularly until she became completely bed-ridden. Now, her bed is drawn up to the window where she can see the church every day. She knows just who is missing from its services on Sunday, and who went to the jumble sale!

There is more to it than that though. Mary says, " Now I can't go and listen to the minister, that building is a sermon in stone to me." There's the steeple pointing heavenwards, the striking of the church clock reminding her of the precious gift of time, the light shining through the stained-glass windows on a winter's night; and so on. All simple things, but they speak to Mary's heart.

The church, for her, is still the centre and inspiration of her life.

IF thou canst believe, all things are possible to him that believeth.

THE children round about us seem to have re-discovered a game which I remember playing long ago. The idea is to pack as many objects as possible into a match box, and our neighbour's young son Alistair was telling us proudly the other day that he's winning among his pals at the moment with over 100 small objects in his box.

By coincidence the very same day I met a friend who retired from work some months ago and of course I asked him how he was getting on. He gave me the answer I receive so often, " Oh, fine! I don't know how I ever found time to go to work!"

He has found, of course, the secret of true happiness—filling life as full as possible with interest and activity in much the same way that young Alistair has packed his matchbox!

A FRIEND of mine has an " interleaved Bible "—blank pages between the pages of text. On those pages he writes his own thoughts and comments and sometimes quotations which seem appropriate to a particular passage in the Bible.

Alongside Jesus's words, " First the blade, then the ear and after that the full corn in the ear," he copied these words by an anonymous writer: " Nature knows no hurry. Only man brought it into the world . . . Nothing happens any more at that leisurely pace at which flowers grow, deer browse, rivers wend their way. Force yourself to go slowly. Maturity takes time, whether it be fruits, states, or great ideas."

Advice which would benefit us all in this often hectic world.

DO you remember that character drawn by Charles Dickens—Mrs Jellyby? She was " full of good works ", but they all centred on Borrioboola-Gha in Africa! Her home was a shambles, her children neglected, her household duties most slatternly performed. She was more interested in things far away than in things close at hand.

Few of us are likely to go as far as Mrs Jellyby did in this respect and, of course, in these days we cannot cut ourselves off from the needs of the wider world, yet it is all too easy sometimes to have a blind-spot about the needs and opportunities which lie all about us.

As John Keble wrote:

> *The daily round, the trivial task,*
> *Will furnish all we ought to ask.*
> *Room to deny ourselves; a road*
> *To bring us, daily, nearer God.*

A FRIEND of ours who has become very deaf started to go to lip-reading classes a little while ago, and is delighted with the results. " Not only can I understand people much more easily but I find that I am looking at people's faces much more carefully now, and what a lot I learn about them by doing that."

Our faces often reflect more about us than we realise. We don't need plastic surgery to improve our faces—our smile, our serenity, our friendliness, our gratitude for life's mercies, are all forces which transfigure the face. The idea of the shining face is no myth. Let ours shine today for the encouragement of others!

FRIDAY—SEPTEMBER 28.

I IMAGINE that William Thackeray's novels are considered a bit old-fashioned these days but there are certainly thoughts in those books which do not date. Take this, for instance, from *Vanity Fair:*

" The world is a looking-glass and gives back to every man the reflection of his own face. Frown at it, and it will in turn look sourly upon you; laugh at it and with it, and it is a jolly, kind companion."

SATURDAY—SEPTEMBER 29.

WHEN on holiday recently the Lady of the House and I attended worship at the local church. One of the most delightful things about the service was to see row upon row of children at the front for the first part of the service.

It reminded me of some words of the Rev. John Harwood, a minister of the United Reformed Church, who built up a very large congregation of children and young people. He loved to see the front pews crowded with them and used to say that a church without children was " like somebody trying to smile without teeth!"

Perhaps an odd simile, but that church we visited would certainly have seemed a less happy place with rows of bare pews at the front. And how many, particularly of the older folk among us, find that not only in church but in our daily life, grandchildren and neighbours' children can often bring the smiles back into our lives.

SUNDAY—SEPTEMBER 30.

HAPPY is the man that findeth wisdom, and the man that getteth understanding.

OCTOBER

MONDAY—OCTOBER 1.

VISITORS to the little village of Bainbridge in North Yorkshire are sometimes surprised (and even startled) to hear, in the evening, the sound of a great bull horn being blown on the village green. On a still night its sound carries over three miles!

For 700 years this custom has been carried out between the Feast of the Holy Rood and Shrovetide. Its purpose was to guide home any foresters who might have lost their way, although there haven't been any forests round Bainbridge for hundreds of years.

Quite apart from the fact that I am always fascinated by the preservation of old customs it seems to me that one like this is a reminder to us that, whatever problems *we* may have, there were perils and trials in the past we do not have to face.

It rather shames my grumbling sometimes when I think of those weary workers making their way home on a winter's night through the dark forests, as I sit comfortably at home.

TUESDAY—OCTOBER 2.

THREE-YEAR-OLD Norman was inquiring where his grandma lived now. After several confusing attempts to get round the question, his mother finally admitted that she was dead.

" Why is she dead?" he asked.

" Because Jesus wanted her with Him," his mother replied.

" Well," he said, in a very matter-of-fact way, " if she is with Jesus she can't be dead."

THE FRIENDSHIP BOOK

WEDNESDAY—OCTOBER 3.

TURNING over the yellowing pages of an old autograph album the other day, I came across one of those anonymous verses written in such books. It went:

At morn he cast his net where fishers were,
At eve he drew it empty to the shore;
He took the diver's plunge into the sea
But thence within his hand no pearl he bore.
He shot an arrow but he missed his mark;
He ran a race but never reached his goal.
Men call it failure; but what if heaven shall question,
Ere her judgment shall be given,
Not, " Hast thou won?" But only, " Hast thou striven?"

THURSDAY—OCTOBER 4.

THE Lady of the House and I have just returned from a windy walk—a little breathless, perhaps, but truly exhilarated! In such circumstances I often think of some words of the writer, Temple Gardiner, when he went out alone one windy night: " A glorious wind was blowing in from the west across the Irish Sea . . . my soul suddenly leaped forth. I felt what a cramped up stuffy life the life of my soul had often been, and I shouted against the wind . . . no-one was there to hear me and I shouted praise in a sort of madness."

That's just how I felt tonight. A soft, gentle breeze can be refreshing, but sometimes we need the thrill of the tempest. *My* song as we battled against the wind was:

O winds of God, awake and blow
The mists of earth away.

THE FRIENDSHIP BOOK

VISITORS to the little church at Harwarden in Clwyd, North Wales, can scarcely miss the beautiful Burne-Jones memorial window to Prime Minister W. E. Gladstone who used to worship there. But I wonder whether they notice in the porch some simple rules for worship which were placed there, I understand, at his suggestion.

The closing words of the notice particularly impressed me: " Be quiet and thoughtful as you go. On your way home be careful of your talk or the world will slip back into your heart."

If that was a danger in more leisurely times, how much more we need the admonition now.

I EXPECT you remember the song " Singing in the Rain " which was made famous by the singing and dancing star, Gene Kelly. Apart from its catchy tune it seems to me to have a valuable philosophy for life. For don't most people, when they say, " It's raining," seem to do so in a rather doleful tone of voice?

How much better to sing with Gene Kelly, or to say, as Margaret Sangster does in her poem " On a Rainy Day ",

> *I think that folk should carry*
> *Bright umbrellas in the rain,*
> *To smile into the sullen sky*
> *And make it glad again.*

TRULY the light is sweet, and a pleasant thing it is for the eyes to behold the sun.

L

MONDAY—OCTOBER 8.

IN one of his volumes of autobiography, J. B. Priestley gives his readers some advice which he always tried to follow himself—" resist what are called ' negative emotions '—blinding anger, envy, jealousy, malice, or even constant worry—because not only do these have a bad effect on character but they are also appalling wasters of energy that could be used for better purposes.

" If I have been energetic in my professional life it is partly because I have largely kept these negative emotions at bay."

Wise words.

TUESDAY—OCTOBER 9.

IN the latter part of the 19th century, the parish of Morwenstow in Cornwall had a somewhat eccentric vicar, the Rev Robert Stephen Hawker. He was often seen about the parish in the strangest clothes, he built a vicarage for himself with chimneys that looked like church towers, and he held services to which he invited cats and dogs to bring their owners!

No doubt when, in October 1843, he decorated his church with fruit and vegetables and invited his congregation to " give thanks for the fruits of harvest " it was considered just another of the vicar's eccentricities. But in fact the idea caught on and spread rapidly so that in a few years' time Harvest Festivals were among the most popular of church services.

So we can forgive Parson Hawker his oddities and remember him for helping to institute one of our most joyful and moving services.

" Come, ye thankful people, come, raise the song of harvest home."

THE FRIENDSHIP BOOK

ALTHOUGH the architect, Sir Edwin Lutyens, is probably best-known to many people for his Cenotaph in Whitehall, London, he was also famous for his designs for country houses and his restoration of old buildings.

He once said, " The best buildings are built slowly " and a fine example of this is his Castle Drogo in Devon, a granite building towering 900 feet above the wooded gorge of the River Teign. It took him 20 years to build—a monument to his philosophy of care and patience, building long and building to last.

The castle is now in the care of the National Trust and though it is a long way for many of us to go, sometimes when I tend to be caught up in the rush and hassle of life I like to look at a picture of Castle Drogo and recall Lutyens' quiet philosophy.

BRUCE was a Welfare Officer in a deprived area. There he befriended a boy named Andy, who came from a very bad family background. Everything seemed stacked against him and yet, said Bruce, Andy never saw it that way.

" I'm going to clear out of here when I'm older," he used to tell Bruce. " I'll get myself a job and work my way up. Some day I'm going to have a lovely house with a garden!"

" Only a dream," some people might say—but Bruce tells me he used to encourage Andy to talk about it and to believe in it.

And he was right. I can't tell you if Andy's dreams came true, but if they did I think Bruce had a lot to do with it—simply because he was willing to listen and to share the hopes of a poor boy.

A FRIEND in America occasionally sends me a copy of *The War Cry*—the Salvation Army magazine there. Some time ago a filler at the bottom of a column caught my eye. It read: " The prayers of good men and women can do more than all the armies and navies of the nation. Prayercraft is greater than aircraft."

An encouraging thought and one I shall long remember.

SATURDAY—OCTOBER 13.

WINDSOR GUILDHALL has a most curious feature—a row of columns down the centre of the hall which do not quite reach the ceiling. The story is that originally it had pillars round the sides only but the councillors expressed the fear that these would not be strong enough. They asked Sir Christopher Wren, the architect of the building, to supply the extra ones. This he agreed to do, but instructed the masons that the pillars should not quite reach the roof, thus justifying his first plan. And the roof still stands!

In some people, of course, an act of that sort might be counted as arrogance, but Wren had confidence in his own work; what he did was done as well as he could possibly do it. And we can apply his principles and integrity to our own work, however humble.

SUNDAY—OCTOBER 14.

A PROPHET is not without honour, but in his own country, and among his own kin, and in his own house.

A NDREW MARVELL, the 17th century poet, was also, for a period, a Member of Parliament. He was a fearless critic of corruption in Court circles and was once approached in his home by a courtier with the clear intention of bribing him to keep silence over a certain matter.

Marvell called his servant. " What is for dinner today, John?" he asked.

" Well sir, there is some mutton."

" And tomorrow?"

The servant looked surprised but said, " Well, it will be the same, if any is left over."

" So," said Marvell, turning to his visitor, " my dinner is provided for today and tomorrow. What need do I have of your money. Good day to you, sir!"

A NEIGHBOUR of mine has green fingers. His cabbages always seem to be twice as big, his peas as high again as mine!

" How do you do it, Alistair?" I asked him.

" Ah, well," he said with a twinkle in his eye, "You see those rows of seeds—you notice I have put a stick at the end of each, with the seed packet stuck on . . ."

" So you will know what you have sown where," I ventured.

" Oh, not just that," he said. " As I put the packet on, with the picture turned towards the row of seeds I say, ' Now, you little blighters, *that's* what I want you to look like!' "

Alistair's quip set me thinking. How much better we would be at many things if we always aimed at the highest and best!

THE FRIENDSHIP BOOK

THE actor David Kossoff has known deep personal grief. His younger son died some years ago in tragic circumstances. But he can still write these inspiring words which I came on in the " Sunday Bulletin ":

" I feel gratitude every day of my life, for simple things usually. The colours of the seasons, the new life of spring, the silver sunlight on a morning hillside, the sheer beauty of the countryside. Bird-song, moonlight, quiet water, healthy children, a quiet mind, a good night's sleep. So much, so much . . . "

A YOUNG man who was an amateur artist, but who had to spend most of his time living and working in a city, often resented his drab surroundings and longed for the freedom and beauty of the countryside.

One day, as he walked down a narrow alley, a gleam of sunlight burst through a gap in the buildings, illuminating a tiny, dirty, but golden-haired, child playing with a doll on a doorstep. Here was a picture indeed! In that moment he made a resolution: every day on the way to work he would try to find at least one subject for a picture.

To his amazement, what had formerly seemed dull and unattractive streets became alive with " pictures "—children playing, clothes on a line fluttering in the breeze, a pot of flowers on a window-sill, some antique railings casting a shadow in the sunlight—the inspiration was endless.

We may not be budding artists, but it won't do us any harm to keep an eye open for the glory in the commonplace!

A MINISTER friend tells me an amusing story of a new but keen member of his church who, at the Annual Church Meeting, questioned an item in the Statement of Accounts: "Pulpit Supplies—£60", referring, of course, to the cost of providing preachers during the minister's absence. Unfortunately, the new member did not understand this.

"It seems an awful lot of money to spend on pulpit supplies," he complained. "I have looked in the pulpit a few times on Sunday mornings and there never seems anything there except a glass of water!"

NOT long ago, the Lady of the House and I attended a fascinating lecture illustrated by slides on the subject of "Walls" in which the speaker talked about the city walls of York and Chester, Hadrian's Wall, the Great Wall of China, the Wailing Wall in Jerusalem and many others, showing how much of our history is bound up in walls.

Then, as his lecture drew to a close, he said, "But this is my favourite wall . . ." And he showed us a picture of his own house! Nor did he need to remind us of those words in Helen Taylor's song, "Bless this House":

> *Bless these walls, so firm and stout,*
> *Keeping want and trouble out.*

I'm sure we all went back within the walls of our own homes with a new and deeper sense of gratitude.

FEAR God, and keep his commandments: for this is the whole duty of man.

MONDAY—OCTOBER 22.

HAVE you heard this prayer before?

It was put together by an Indian Jain priest named Satish Kuma, and first used at a service in Westminster Abbey:

Lead me from death to life, from falsehood to truth.

Lead me from despair to hope, from fear to trust.

Lead me from hate to love, from war to peace.

Let peace fill our hearts, our world, our universe.

Peace, peace, peace.

The intention is that this prayer should be repeated every day at 12 noon. If for some reason you are too busy at 12 noon where you live, it is worth remembering that it is always 12 noon somewhere in God's wide world, and that " the voice of prayer is never silent, nor dies the strain of praise away."

TUESDAY—OCTOBER 23.

TWO boys, Archibald Walters and a younger friend, wandered away from their homes one wintry afternoon. When it began to get dark the boys lost their way and decided to shelter under a hedge until daylight.

The younger boy complained of feeling very cold, so Archibald took off all his clothes, except his shirt, and covered the little boy with them. Early next morning a farm labourer found them and took them to a farm where efforts were made to revive them. The younger boy recovered, but Archibald died from exposure.

He is commemorated in the Parish Church at Horfield, Bristol, by a memorial window and a plaque which reads: " To the Glory of God in memory of the boy hero Archibald Walters who gave his life to save his friend. October 23rd 1874."

UNCHANGING

Dynasties may rise and fall
But always there remains the soil
And crops that must be gathered in
Through centuries of ceaseless toil.

MY heart goes out to the lonely little boy who said wistfully to his mother, "Mummy, I wish I were two little puppies so that I could play together!"

THURSDAY—OCTOBER 25.

TODAY is one of the perhaps lesser-known saints' days—that of St. Crispin and St. Crispinian. According to ancient tradition they were brothers who came in the third century from Rome to Soissons in France where they worked as Christian missionaries, earning their living as shoemakers and where they were eventually martyred. They became the patron saints of shoemakers and leather workers.

All of which reminds me of John Potter who, more than 50 years ago, was a clogmaker in Cumberland. He worked by day in his workshop surrounded by the tools of his trade but his evenings were spent in a book-lined room above his shop, reading the classics and writing poetry.

When someone remarked that it seemed an unusual combination he shrugged his shoulders and said quietly, " Even a pair of clogs is like a poem to me!" A philosophy not far from that of Crispin and Crispinian.

FRIDAY—OCTOBER 26.

RITA SNOWDEN'S books such as " When I Open My Door ", " Through Open Windows ", and " The Wind Blows ", must have brought inspiration to many. At a time of crisis these words of hers have helped many: " Life's sweet secret for us is a dual secret—knowing when to go back and remember, and when to go forward and forget."

THE FRIENDSHIP BOOK

A RED INDIAN and a white man were walking through a town together. The Red Indian suddenly stopped and said, " I can hear a little animal."

The white man laughed. " I hear nothing."

" Look," said the Indian, and gently parted the leaves of a creeper to reveal a tiny cricket.

" Well," said the white man, " you Indians have far sharper hearing than we have."

" Not at all," said the Indian, and dropped a small coin. Immediately a bunch of white children appeared, and grovelled on their knees to find it. " We just hear different things."

D AUGHTER, thy faith hath made thee whole; go in peace.

A STOCKHOLM doctor whose hobby is photography has told of a very interesting experiment he made. He took photographs of human faces and found that if he superimposed 14 or more photos on top of each other the resulting face was always beautiful. However many times he tried his experiment the result was always the same—beauty!

We don't need a camera to work this experiment. If we look at individual people with individual experiences, we often find unpleasant things, but when we add *all* our experiences together, when we see life as a whole, what beauty and goodness is there! Let's not be put off by a bit of unpleasantness here and there. The overall picture of life is truly beautiful.

THE stories we hear about the 19th century Italian patriot, Garibaldi, are usually about his courage as a soldier and his greatness as a leader, but there was another and perhaps unexpected side to his character.

Late one evening as he and his men were returning to their quarters they met a shepherd looking for a lost lamb. They all went off searching in different directions and Garibaldi's men lost touch with their leader and eventually returned without him.

Next morning Garibaldi's servant was surprised to find him fast asleep long after he was usually up and about. The servant's movements disturbed Garibaldi and he woke up. Then, reaching down under the bed clothes Garibaldi brought out the lost lamb. He had found it, half-dead with cold, and revived it in the warmth of his own bed.

LOOKING up a passage recently in my dictionary of quotations I came upon some words by Elizabeth Bibesco. I confess she is a writer unknown to me, but I think we would all be a lot richer in the truest sense of the word if we remembered what she said:

" I have made a great discovery. What I love belongs to me. Not just the chairs and tables in my house, but the masterpieces of the world. It is only a question of loving them enough."

When you think of it, there are lots of things we can never possess in a physical sense but which are truly " ours " if we have a deep love for them in our hearts; and no-one can rob us of those possessions.

NOVEMBER

THURSDAY—NOVEMBER 1.

IN one of his books Dr F. W. Boreham tells the story of an old priest who was trudging home through deep snow after early Mass on All Saints Day. A man stopped him to ask how many had been at his service.

" Millions!" replied the old priest. " Millions!"

Today is All Saints Day in the calendar of the Christian Church and for many of us life would seem much poorer if we did not feel ourselves, as the writer of the letter to the Hebrews says, to be " compassed about with so great a cloud of witnesses." We are part of a great army.

FRIDAY—NOVEMBER 2.

WHEN the Lady of the House and I were on holiday we had the pleasure of something which many of us nowadays, in these times of central heating and smokeless zones, rarely experience—a log fire burning in the hearth! How nostalgic the fragrance! It reminded me of an old poem, part of which went,

> *Pear logs and apple logs,*
> *They will scent your room;*
> *Cherry logs across the dogs*
> *Smell like flowers in bloom.*

And while I am in this nostalgic mood I recall, too, G. K. Chesterton's words: " A queer fancy seems to be current that a fire exists only to warm people. It exists also to light their darkness, to raise their spirits, to toast their muffins, to air their rooms, to cook their chestnuts, to tell stories to their children, to make chequered shadows on their walls . . . "

SATURDAY—NOVEMBER 3.

WILLIAM ENGLISH was the first manager of the Cheshire Lines railway. He had many amusing stories to tell, including the one about the time he was travelling on one of his own trains between Manchester and Chester. An Irish ticket collector looked into the carriage to check the tickets.

The manager smiled at him. " I'm English," he said.

" It doesn't matter whether you're English or Irish," said the ticket collector, " You must pay the fare or out you go!"

SUNDAY—NOVEMBER 4.

THE path of the just is as the shining light, that shineth more and more unto the perfect day.

MONDAY—NOVEMBER 5.

THE gardens of Levens Hall in Cumbria contain a remarkable collection of topiary work—trees cut into a great variety of shapes: pyramids, spirals and arches, as well as figures of people and animals.

The man who created the gardens was a Frenchman, M. Guillaume Beaumont, who came to Levens in 1690. Many wealthy land-owners tried to tempt him away but he had a vision of what Levens could become with long, patient, painstaking work and he chose to spend the last 40 years of his life there turning his vision into reality.

The gardens are said to be the only ones in England which have remained virtually unchanged since that period, so M. Beaumont has left a lasting mark upon the scene—as patience and application always do in the lives of all of us.

THE FRIENDSHIP BOOK

THE Jews treasure a collection of writings called The Talmud which was completed during the early centuries of the Christian era, and to which about 2,000 authors contributed.

Here is an example of its wisdom which I copied down into one of my notebooks many years ago:

" There are ten strong things. Iron is strong, but fire melts it. Fire is strong, but water quenches it. Water is strong but the clouds evaporate it. Clouds are strong, but winds drive them away. Man is strong, but fears cast him down. Fear is strong but sleep overcomes it. Sleep is strong, yet death is stronger. Death is strong, but loving-kindness survives death."

THE Lady of the House and I called on Mrs Andrews, for many years deputy organist at her church. A recent stroke put an end to this, having left her paralysed down the right side.

To my astonished admiration I found that Mrs Andrews had already taught herself to sew with her left hand and was busy working at a tapestry firescreen.

" Do you know, I almost dreaded visiting Mrs Andrews," I later confessed to my wife. " I wondered how such an active person would cope with her disability."

" Surely you know there are two ways of meeting adversity," the Lady of the House replied. " You either admit defeat or you press on and win a victory."

As one of life's overcomers, Mrs Andrews is an inspiration to everyone who knows her.

THURSDAY—NOVEMBER 8.

DOROTHY GRAY was very fond of animals and did much good work for them. She wrote this lovely poem which she titled " The Birth Of A Dog ":

When the Maker was resting from labour,
*   As He gazed on the world from above,*
He saw many poor lonely humans
*   With no one to care for and love.*
And the Lord in His infinite mercy,
*   With compassion both tender and wise,*
Made a furry and four-legged creature
*   With a tail and a pair of brown eyes . . .*
And a heart filled with loyal devotion
*   From the moment his short life began.*
And the Maker smiled down from His heaven
*   On the DOG He created for Man.*

FRIDAY—NOVEMBER 9.

GOSSIP, as we all know, can be very harmful and damaging. I like these promises once written down by John Wesley:

" We will not listen to or willingly inquire after any ill concerning each other."

" If we do hear any ill of each other we will not be forward to believe it."

" As soon as possible we will communicate what we hear by speaking or writing to the person concerned."

" Till we have done this we will not write or speak a syllable of it to any other person whatever."

" Neither will we mention it after we have done this, to any other person."

" We will not make any exception to any of these rules unless we think ourselves absolutely obliged in conscience so to do."

TOIL

Some work is hard and testing,
  Demanding strength and skill,
But always there are hardy men
  To labour with a will.

M

THE FRIENDSHIP BOOK

FROM time to time a friend of mine visits a remote farm to absorb the peace and calm of the countryside. He learns much from the philosophy of the farmer who has come to terms with the vagaries of flocks, crops, and weather.

During a recent drought, which caused a fair amount of concern, the farmer merely said: " Why worry? The land will adjust. It always has done, and it always will."

He has learned the secret of contentment and a quiet mind. No wonder my friend always returns from his visits to the farm feeling refreshed in body and soul.

SUNDAY—NOVEMBER 11.

EVEN the Son of man came not to be ministered unto, but to minister, and to give his life a ransom for many.

MONDAY—NOVEMBER 12.

I WAS admiring the obviously new tie which a friend was wearing, but I was a little puzzled when he said, " It's an un-birthday present from my Aunt Annie!"

He went on to explain that his aunt didn't give people presents on their birthdays on principle. She held that they would get enough presents then and thought it was better to give a present as a surprise when they were not expecting it.

It may sound a little bit eccentric, but I am sure it must bring a lot of happiness both in the giving and receiving, for giving and receiving pleasant surprises can brighten up life no end for all of us, can't it?

TUESDAY—NOVEMBER 13.

SOME people are too modest. I don't know who " Grimes " is, but under that pen-name, in a little brochure called " The Link ", which tells what is happening among the mentally handicapped in Scotland, he described how, for ten years, he had been taking a bus-load of youngsters to the nearest swimming pool—which happens to be 15 miles away.

On a winter night, when roads are icy and the fireside warm, it can be a bit of an effort. But what rewards there are!

When, for instance, after weeks of splashing, John lets go of the rail and ventures into the middle of the bath.

When Marion, who had been a very disturbed teenager, not only learns to swim but spends a whole evening teaching—successfully—a frightened small boy from a very deprived family to take his first strokes across the pool.

" Yes, it's all worth while," says Grimes. To any man or woman whose family have flown, he invites: " Come and join us. The fireside will still be waiting when you are 80!"

WEDNESDAY—NOVEMBER 14.

CONDUCTOR André Previn was once invited to appear as guest pianist with a New York orchestra. He arrived for a rehearsal only to find that someone had failed to provide a piano. Undeterred, Previn rehearsed the entire concert simply tapping on a table top with his fingers.

It is often said, " a poor workman blames his tools." On this occasion Previn was able to demonstrate what could be done by a great artiste even when *deprived* of his tools.

A CATHOLIC, a Protestant and a Jew found themselves in the same platoon during the last war. They became great friends.

One day when they were walking together behind the lines, a stray piece of shrapnel killed the Protestant.

The only place of worship at hand was Catholic, so the Catholic and the Jew went to the priest who told them he could not bury a Protestant on consecrated ground, but promised to bury him as close to it as possible.

When the two friends returned some time later to visit their comrade's grave, they were surprised to find it inside the cemetery fence.

" But," they said to the priest, " this can't be our friend. You told us that you couldn't break the rules."

" It *is* your friend," he replied gently. " I couldn't break the rules—but I could move the fence."

FRIDAY—NOVEMBER 16.

D R FREDERIC LOOMIS, a Canadian, spent a lifetime in obstetrics and gynaecology. During the years he helped many women with different problems, but he never forgot one little old lady who arrived in need of surgery but without any money to pay for it. He made the necessary arrangements, and after her operation spent several hours by her bedside.

Six months later he received from her a package—a pair of fine gloves which she had made herself, and of better quality than any he had ever owned before. With them was a note: " To warm the hands that made me well."

I have no doubt that did warm his hands, and I am sure that touching note warmed his heart as well.

THE FRIENDSHIP BOOK

A DISPENSER retired from his work at a chemist's shop in Hereford. The proprietor explained: " He came to work here 50 years ago for a month to see if he liked it—and now he's decided he doesn't."

FOR what shall it profit a man, if he shall gain the whole world, and lose his own soul?

GEORGE CADBURY was a pioneer of welfare for his work people. In 1860 he and his brother Richard took over their Quaker father's cocoa firm in Birmingham. Times were difficult, but even so the brothers were keenly interested in the welfare of their employees. Two of the earliest social amenities provided were a football and a bone-shaker bicycle.

The business prospered. In the late 1870's the Cadbury brothers bought $14\frac{1}{2}$ acres of the Bournebrook Estate for a new factory. Works councils, one for men, another for women, were introduced and these proved invaluable, for here workers could voice their own ideas and hear management problems—a little-known thing in the 19th century. But George was inspired with another scheme—that of a garden village, housing workers and providing them with leisure facilities. In 1893 another 120 acres were bought and the model village built.

When George Cadbury died, the works councils sent a message to his family which included the tribute: " His life cannot help but inspire us all to nobler lives and greater deeds of service."

TUESDAY—NOVEMBER 20.

AN artist was showing a friend round his studio which was packed with his paintings. The friend looked admiringly at them all and then said, " Which do *you* think is the best of all your paintings here?"

The artist led him across to a corner of the studio and, pointing, said, " That one!" It was a blank canvas—the picture he had not yet done but which he hoped would be the best ever!

As the poet Robert Browning said, " The best is yet to be."

WEDNESDAY—NOVEMBER 21.

EBENEZER MATHER was a Londoner who worked in the Thames Church Mission. He knew a fair number of seamen, but no fishermen, so one day in 1881 he visited the Dogger Bank on one of their smacks. That brief trip changed his life.

He bought a fishing smack and turned it into a sea-going shop, church, library and hospital. Tobacco was cheap, mittens and mufflers were given free, and Bibles were readily available.

Every Sunday morning Mather would preach a simple Gospel message through a loud-hailer from his boat to a congregation of fishermen gathered in their boats round him. By 1885 Ebenezer Mather had five boats operating in the North Sea. Today, the service is still maintained in 20 centres, most of them in Scotland, but including others as far south as Cornwall. They offer recreational and canteen facilities, a Sunday service, and sometimes sleeping accommodation or a sick bay.

We know it as the Royal National Mission to Deep Sea Fishermen, and countless men have had cause to be grateful to Ebenezer Mather.

THE FRIENDSHIP BOOK

THE Welsh love of music and song is known to us all and I was interested to read recently in an article about the Welsh harp that a 12th century Welsh law stated that any of a person's possessions could be seized for debt except his harp, so great was the store set by music.

Today is the festival day of Cecilia, patron saint of music. The poet, Joseph Addison, wrote " A Song for St. Cecilia's Day " in which he said,

Music, the greatest good that mortals know,
And all of heaven we have below.

Many of us would say " Amen " to that, and we might well start this St Cecilia's Day by humming our favourite tune to ourselves!

MORE than 100 years ago Lord Sandys was served an excellent sauce in a Bombay restaurant. He asked for the recipe, which he brought back to England. He later requested Lea and Perrin to make it up for him but, in spite of several attempts, Lord Sandys was disappointed with the results. Lea and Perrin eventually admitted defeat and stowed a barrel of sauce away in a cellar.

Many months later, the sauce was discovered, tasted, and found to have a delicious flavour. Time had done its work and Worcester Sauce was born.

We live in an age geared to ever increasing speed, where instant mashed potato, instant cake mixes and instant coffee are part of our life style.

I cannot help thinking that we miss many of the good things of life by being in such a hurry. Isn't there still something to be said for the once prized virtue of patience?

VESPERS

Children, happy as the day,
Whose natures blossom in the light,
If they have been taught to pray
Will never fear the darkest night.

THE FRIENDSHIP BOOK

DID you hear the story about the two friends, Mrs X and Mrs Y, who fell out one day and stopped speaking to one another?

After a few weeks of simmering ill-feeling Mrs X decided to go round to Mrs Y's house and " have it out " with her. She marched up to Mrs Y's front door and banged on the knocker as hard as she dared, all the while practising the sort of speech that could make even a politician quake and tremble.

Then the door opened and there stood Mrs Y smiling and holding out both hands in welcome. " Come along in," she said. " I've been hoping for a chance to sort out our little differences over a cuppa."

Mrs X was so flabbergasted that she completely forgot all the nasty things she'd planned to say. " It was the smile that did it," she said afterwards.

Which just goes to prove that a smile can work miracles.

A SOFT answer turneth away wrath: but grievous words stir up anger.

A FRIEND of ours told us about going to church a few weeks before Christmas when the ceremony of lighting the Advent Candles was taking place. As a member of the congregation lit the candle a child's voice broke the silence, singing, " Happy Birthday to You!"

Not surprisingly, the congregation laughed, yet what could be more appropriate? " Out of the mouths of babes . . ."

I WAS interested to read in an article about ancient mosaic work that the workmen engaged in creating these designs did not always know what the finished mosaic would be like. Sometimes it depended on what materials were available and what ideas came into their minds as they worked. They were not, as I had always thought, working to a carefully planned design.

There is encouragement in the thought that we, too, with patience and imagination, can build the bits and pieces of our lives into something of beauty and usefulness.

WEDNESDAY—NOVEMBER 28.

THE missionary, Dr Stanley Jones, tells in one of his books of a journey by air to India many years ago. In the early morning he left Marseilles and the plane stopped to re-fuel at Corsica. He remembered how, from that island, Napoleon went forth to conquer the world. At noon he lunched at Naples, the land from which the Caesars set out to subdue the earth. At nightfall he was in Greece, from which land Alexander went to be a world conqueror. The next day he flew past Assyria and Babylon, lands from which mighty kings went forth to make the earth tremble.

As he flew over these different countries, he said he was impressed by the fact that every one of those mighty empires is dead and gone. Their once all-powerful leaders are now only names in the history books.

On the other hand, Stanley Jones, as a missionary, felt himself flying in the service of " a kingdom which knows no end ".

ALTHOUGH Tommy Steele has been in the entertainment business for many years he still astonishes his many admirers with his youthful looks and energy. Asked by an interviewer about the secret of this " perpetual youth " he said, " Every night I just look forward to waking up tomorrow and enjoying another day's work. I think that keeps you young."

A fairly simple philosophy, but it obviously works for Tommy Steele, and there is no reason why it should not work for us.

FOR many years Norman Ellison, better known to generations of children as " Nomad the Naturalist," delighted thousands of BBC Children's Hour listeners with his broadcasts about the countryside, its birds and animals, trees and flowers.

Writing about this work, he said, " My quest for fresh material has taken me over most parts of the British Isles, yet many of the incidents I have recounted to this vast unseen audience have happened on my own doorstep on Caldy Hill or around the Hilbre Islands I can see as I write these words."

From the window of his home on the Wirral Peninsula in Cheshire, Nomad could see more than most people see on many a mile of walking. His eye and mind were attuned to the wonder and beauties that lay close at hand.

This idea extends, of course, beyond the world of Nature to the whole of our human experience. There is so much of goodness and gladness close at hand if only we have eyes to see and hearts and minds to appreciate it.

DECEMBER

DURING the American Civil War an ambassador was surprised to find Abraham Lincoln polishing his boots.

"Mr President," he exclaimed. "Do you think that the President of the United States should clean his own boots?"

Abraham Lincoln looked up, and smiled. "Mr Ambassador, if the President does not clean his own boots, whose boots should he clean?"

HE that spareth his rod hateth his son: but he that loveth him chasteneth him betimes.

KATHLEEN MORGAN was awaiting the arrival of a piano and five-year-old Debbie was as impatient as her mother. But Debbie's bedtime was long past before the piano arrived.

As Debbie was fast asleep, her mother thought she would play softly one or two much-loved tunes. Suddenly she noticed a small figure in the doorway.

"Mummy, that was lovely," said Debbie. "I will learn to play the piano tomorrow."

I rather fancy it will take Debbie more than a day to learn to play like her mother, but what a lovely little picture the incident made—Kathleen softly playing and the little girl listening, and wanting to do the same. And with a determination like that, Debbie will do it, too!

THE FRIENDSHIP BOOK

WHAT men need most when things go wrong is not always help, but cheer.

I have been reading a little story told by Dr William Barclay about Mr Gladstone. He once made an important speech in The House of Commons and unfortunately the figures quoted in it were all wrong. They had been given to him by his Parliamentary Secretary. The Opposition shouted with joy—it was a big public humiliation for him.

That same evening Mr Gladstone wrote to his Secretary. Not, as you might expect, a letter of reproval, but a kind letter assuring him that there was no need to worry. " All men make mistakes, the matter will not be mentioned again," wrote the great man.

Mr Gladstone knew well that when a man has made a mistake he will do better with encouragement than reprimand.

HOW many angels can stand on the point of a needle?

Dr William B. Robertson of Irvine had no doubt. " Five," he said.

It seems that one stormy winter night he had been returning home late along a side street when he noticed a light in the window of a room where there lived a poor woman whose husband was a seaman. Dr Robertson knew that her husband had just gone off to sea and, wondering if she was all right, he went in. He found her diligently plying needle and thread whilst her five children lay sound asleep around the room.

" There," declared Dr Robertson with emphasis, " was a needle supporting five angels."

THE FRIENDSHIP BOOK

A FEW years ago, a motorist was driving along a country road, listening to the daily service on the radio, when suddenly his car burst into flames. What could he do? As it happened, the hymn on the radio at that moment was:

> *Oh happy band of pilgrims,*
> *Look upwards to the skies . . .*

He did precisely that—and saw a helicopter descending rapidly. Out came the pilot, fire extinguisher at the ready. Out went the flames. Up and off again went the helicopter before the motorist had time to remember the next two lines of the hymn:

> *Where such a light affliction*
> *Shall win you such a prize.*

Well, *was* it just coincidence, or was the hymn true for him?

E VERYTHING in my life has a price, but nothing has any value," a pop star said on a television interview.

I was about to turn the programme off but that sentence arrested my attention. The screen showed a palatial house where the star never felt at home. He possessed a fleet of cars, but had nowhere special to go. His marriage had foundered.

That lonely, disillusioned man's words still rang in my ears when the Lady of the House brought me my favourite nightcap—a steaming cup of cocoa.

As I drank it I looked at our cat curled up on the rug. In companionable silence we watched the dying embers and I felt deeply grateful for a house that is truly a home. Here I enjoy loving care, comfort and peace—things without price but of how great a value.

THE FRIENDSHIP BOOK

A FRIEND in Nottingham tells me that a certain small girl announced to her parents:

" I know what Santa Claus's real name is—it's Stan."

" How do you know?" asked her mother.

" Well," she replied, " when I was getting my toy from him in the grotto, a lady came up to Santa and said, ' There's a cup of tea in the back for you, Stan.' "

H E that hath ears to hear, let him hear.

A S I watched the Lady of the House rummaging through a box of what she calls her " bits and pieces " I was reminded of an article I read years ago by Howard Corey about the things which people keep. He put them in categories which went something like this: Things that go on things (lids, caps from bottles); Things that come off things (buttons, buckles, hinges, nuts off bolts); Things too nice to use, and Things it seems a shame to throw away!

How many of us recognise ourselves as being hoarders of one sort or another mentioned there?

I hope we are hoarders of other things, too—of friendships, of good books we have read, of happy memories, of beautiful places we have visited, of kind words spoken to us and thoughtful deeds done for us, of music that has gladdened us, of worship that has inspired us.

What a lot there is worth keeping!

BROWSING round a museum recently, the Lady of the House and I came across a fascinating collection of tea caddies. Some of them were made of wood, beautifully inlaid in many cases. Others were metal, finely wrought and colourfully decorated. But most interesting to us were two with locks on them!

There are lots of things we think of locking up nowadays, but not our tea! We forget that it was once a prized and costly commodity. In the 18th century it could cost as much as 18/- per pound—a lot of money then—so it was worth locking up.

I came away pondering how many things we take for granted nowadays, things we regard as very ordinary, which were once luxuries confined to the use of the few and wealthy. A little thought to make us realise how very fortunate we are.

ONE of the wisest men of olden times was Brother Lawrence, who believed he was serving God as much by washing dishes faithfully as by doing some far greater task. He had not always believed this. For many years he longed to do something great in God's service. But then, as he did his menial job it came to him that if God wanted him to work in the kitchen, then he would do it to God's glory. As he worked, he prayed. He is reputed to have said:

" All things are possible to him who believes. They are less difficult to him who hopes. They are easy to him who loves. And they are simple to him who does all three."

His little book, *The Practice of the Presence of God,* has helped thousands of Christians whose work sometimes seems humdrum.

CREATION

There's a special joy in making,
  Bringing life to wood and stone,
And a humble pleasure knowing
  That the work is all our own.

THURSDAY—DECEMBER 13.

WHO was Scrooge? Ask almost anyone and they will tell you he was a miser, a miserable old curmudgeon. Yet, in a way, to say that is to miss the whole point of Dickens's story, for, by the end of " The Christmas Carol " he is a generous and kindly man. Sadly, no-one ever seems to remember this when they talk about him—he's still the miserly old Scrooge they met at the beginning of the story! Poor old Scrooge—he doesn't get the credit he deserves.

It's so easy to condemn, to remember the worst in people. I think we all have one or two Scrooges in our lives—people we see only in a bad light. Perhaps they made a mistake once. Let's not keep it up against them. It's the Scrooge at the *end* of the book that matters, not the one at the beginning.

FRIDAY—DECEMBER 14.

EVERYONE'S definition of a friend is different, but probably akin in some manner. One good description I heard was, " Someone who knows the worst, but who continues to believe the best of one."

Most people are rich in having three or four true friends like that.

One attribute is especially necessary in a friend—loyalty.

William Penn, the old Quaker who ventured from Buckinghamshire to found the new American state of Pennsylvania said: " A true friend unbosoms freely, assists readily, adventures boldly, takes all patiently, defends courageously and continues a friend unchangingly. The covetous, the angry, the proud, the jealous, the talkative cannot but make ill friends."

While Emerson believes that a true friend recognises a person's potential and encourages it.

FOUR-YEAR-OLD Jonathan, picking up one of the family's Christmas cards depicting the infant Jesus in His crib, commented: " Why, He was in His cradle last year—I thought He'd have been walking by now."

WHOSOEVER will save his life shall lose it; but whosoever shall lose his life for my sake and the gospel's, the same shall save it.

ONE Monday morning a young man called to see his mother who lived alone. " Did you go to church yesterday, Mother?" he asked.

" Yes, of course," was the reply.

" And what was the text?"

His mother pondered but could not remember.

" Well, what was the sermon about?" he persisted. But she could not remember that either—though it had been a very good sermon, she said.

" It doesn't seem much good going to church if you can't remember anything about it, does it?"

His mother did not answer the question but took up a wicker basket and said, " John, do me a favour while you are here will you? Take this basket and fill it at the tap."

" Come, Mother," he laughed. " I am not as stupid as that! There wouldn't be a drop of water in the basket when I got back."

" No," replied his mother quietly. " But the basket would be cleaner, wouldn't it?"

TUESDAY—DECEMBER 18.

MY old friend John is not a very good singer. In fact, he himself admits he is a bit croaky. But that doesn't prevent him making a joyful noise to the Lord in church.

"A minister summed it all up for me years ago," he said. "He once told me, 'Some of us sing like crows and some like nightingales, but as long as there are more nightingales than crows we needn't worry'."

John chuckled. "I reckon we have more nightingales than crows in our church so I just carry on."

I thought this little story might encourage some shy folk to follow John's example.

WEDNESDAY—DECEMBER 19.

THE familiar Christmas carol "Good King Wenceslas" reminds us that the snow lay round about, deep and crisp and even . . .

Most of us hate having to trudge through the snow, and yet under two feet of snow, scientists tell us that the temperature is 40 degrees warmer than above it! The snow forms a warm blanket for the earth, and in cold climates farmers depend on the snow to keep the hard frosts off their sown crops. Underneath the snow, beautiful flowers have been found growing that would have perished in much milder climates if exposed to the air; and in the Alps some lovely flowers grow on the edge of the snow-fields.

It is one of the wonders of life that the much-maligned snow makes the earth underneath very much warmer than on top, so that growing things appreciate it even if we don't!

WINTER BEAUTY

THURSDAY—DECEMBER 20.

MRS CHRISTINE WOOD of Surbiton has told me of a Christmas she specially remembers. On the Sunday before Christmas Day she distributed sugar mice, crayons and chocolate coins to the children in her Sunday School class. They surprised her by giving her presents in return—a hand-painted calendar, carefully sewn comb-case, a knitted kettle-holder, a raffia mat and so on. Her throat tightened and she suddenly felt ashamed.

Those children had put patient, loving work into their gifts, thereby giving her something of themselves. All she had done was to give hastily bought presents.

" I had even begrudged the time it took to wrap them, yet I had had the temerity to talk to those children about Christmas being a giving time," she writes. " They taught me what true giving was really all about and I've never forgotten their lesson."

FRIDAY—DECEMBER 21.

THERE are patron saints for children, for travellers, for many trades, for sailors and even for the EEC (St Benedict), but did you know that there is a saint specially concerned with the elderly? He is St Thomas whose festival day is today, and I think it is very fitting that the elderly should be remembered so near to Christmas.

In years gone by, this day was the traditional occasion for gifts to the aged poor—food, warm clothing, blankets, and so on. If we ourselves are elderly let us make this day one of thanksgiving for the blessings we have and if we are younger perhaps we can make it the occasion of some special act of thoughtfulness and concern for an older person.

THE FRIENDSHIP BOOK

IN 1938 the founder of the Ford Motor Company and his wife celebrated their Golden Wedding.

Not surprisingly, he was asked, " What is the key to your successful marriage?" Henry Ford's reply came with simple honesty: " The formula is the same that I always used in making cars—just stick to one model."

His Model-T, produced to make possible cheap and reliable motoring for the millions, sold over 15 million vehicles between 1908 and 1927, and in his marriage Henry Ford was also richly blessed.

And who can say his formula doesn't work?

YE shall find the babe wrapped in swaddling clothes, lying in a manger.

IN Mexico it is the custom on Christmas Eve to take a gift to church. There is a legend that long ago, a poor Mexican boy was broken-hearted because he had no gift to take. Kneeling on the ground, he prayed that God would provide him with something. When he had finished his prayer he opened his eyes and the first thing he saw was a bright red bush by the wayside. Eagerly he broke off some of the branches and ran with them to church.

The bush was the poinsettia which, over the past 25 years or so, has become an increasingly popular feature of our Christmas decorations. But I like its Mexican name—" Flower of the Holy Night " — which reminds us of the old legend and says something to us all on Christmas Eve.

THE FRIENDSHIP BOOK

A S most of us know, the name Santa Claus comes from St Nicholas, the patron saint of children. But until I read Frank and Jamie Muir's book, " A Treasury of Christmas " I did not realise how many other groups of people claim him as their patron saint. They include travellers, brokers, boatmen, dockers, coopers, parish clerks, pawnbrokers, brewers, pilgrims, Russia, the city of Aberdeen and those who have unjustly lost law suits!

This surely is a reminder to us that Christmas is for everybody—wise men and shepherds, young and old, rich and poor, sad and joyful. If only we will listen, Christmas has a word for us all.

W ILFRED SHEPHERD was a Methodist minister whose church was almost in the shadow of Carlisle Cathedral and he spent many hours wandering round that historic building. He used to say, " He who has seen a cathedral a hundred times has undoubtedly seen something, whereas he who has seen a hundred cathedrals has seen nothing at all."

I have met visitors from other lands rushing round this country on a seven-day tour, or something of the sort—seeing everything, yet seeing nothing, really.

Of course, it is a good thing to widen our knowledge and experience but I wonder sometimes whether we don't miss much of the wonder which lies in the familiar, in the things and places close at hand. Let's look—and look again—at our surroundings. There's little doubt that we shall see something we have never noticed before!

IN HARMONY

Before the sunglow's splendour
There is a sense beyond our measure
Of nature's boundless majesty—
A rich reward for us to treasure,
Made richer when a friend is by,
For pleasure shared is double pleasure.

THURSDAY—DECEMBER 27.

I REMEMBER a rather argumentative old fellow who, when he had made some rather controversial statement, had a habit of saying, " Tell me if I'm wrong." The thing was that he did not like it at all if people *did* tell him when he was wrong! He was quite unable to take criticism—something that perhaps few of us, in fact, find easy.

How different was the case of that great Bible translator and martyr who died praying, " Lord open the King of England's eyes." For all his scholarship Tyndale never thought himself infallible. In the preface to his 1534 translation he wrote: " Where they find faults, let them show it to me if they be nigh, or write to me if they be far off, or write openly against it, and I promise that, if I perceive that their reasons conclude, I will confess mine ignorance openly."

One of Dr William Barclay's prayers goes: " Make me humble enough to know my faults and, if I can't see them myself, to listen to others when they tell me about them."

FRIDAY—DECEMBER 28.

THE end of a year makes us very conscious of the passage of time. It is a fitting occasion to recall and ponder the words of the American writer and preacher, Henry van Dyke:

> *Time is:*
> *Too slow for those who wait,*
> *Too swift for those who fear,*
> *Too long for those who grieve,*
> *Too short for those who rejoice,*
> *But for those who love, Time is*
> *Eternity.*

THE FRIENDSHIP BOOK

ON the vestibule wall of the Methodist Church, Southey Street, Keswick, are these lines:

If after Church you wait awhile,
Someone greets you with a smile;
But if you quickly rise and flee,
We'll all seem cold and stiff, maybe.
The one beside you in the pew
Perhaps is just a stranger, too.
All here, like you, have fears and cares,
All of us need each other's prayers;
In fellowship we bid you meet
With us, around God's mercy seat.

WATCH ye and pray, lest ye enter into temptation. The spirit truly is ready, but the flesh is weak.

LOOK now forward and let the backward be." This is not exactly an original thought for the end of the Old Year or the beginning of the New, but I heard it in a television programme in which Malcolm Muggeridge spoke to Josef Stalin's daughter, Svetlana, about her life in Russia, her conversion to Christianity, her defection from the atheistic state and her subsequent life in India and America, and it seemed especially significant.

If, in the dramatic and often desperate circumstances of her life, Svetlana could learn to forget the past and look to the future how much more ought we to be able to do so.

A hopeful New Year to you!

Where the Photographs were taken

PLACE OF PRAYER — *Wells Cathedral, Somerset.*

FRIENDLY LIGHT — *Beachy Head, East Sussex.*

LISTEN — *near Seilebost, South Harris.*

OLD ORDER — *Cleeve Abbey, Somerset.*

GIVE THANKS — *Naunton, Devon.*

LAKELAND IDYLL — *Derwentwater, Cumbria.*

COME IN! — *Tavistock, Devon.*

IF ONLY . . . — *The Old Mill, Christchurch, Dorset.*

GREEN THOUGHTS — *Savill Gardens, Windsor Great Park, Berkshire.*

BREEZE OF MORNING — *Loweswater, Cumbria.*

GOLDEN HOURS — *Brompton Beck, near Pickering, N. Yorkshire.*

UNCHANGING — *St Michael's Mount, Cornwall.*

IN HARMONY — *Oban, Argyll.*

Printed and Published by D. C. Thomson & Co. Ltd.,
185 Fleet Street, London EC4A 2HS.

© D. C. Thomson & Co. Ltd., 1983.

ISBN 0 85116 292 4